THE SUGAR-DETOX COOKBOOK
FOR BEGINNERS

Delicious Sugar-Free Recipes and Expert Tips for Optimal
Blood Sugar Levels, Satisfying Cravings, and
Enjoying Your Favorite Food to the Fullest

ELOISE HEWITT

TABLE OF CONTENT

INTRODUCTION

Let's Start Talking About Glucose

Glucose is a simple sugar that is used by many living things, including humans, to get energy. It is otherwise called dextrose and is a monosaccharide, meaning it is comprised of a solitary sugar particle. In plants, the process of photosynthesis produces glucose, and in humans and animals, the digestion of food carbohydrates provides glucose.

Once consumed, glucose is shipped through the circulation system to the cells of the body, where it is utilized in different metabolic processes. When glucose levels in the bloodstream are low, excess glucose can be broken down and used for energy by the liver and muscles as glycogen.

It is essential to keep in mind that the body also makes use of glucose as a building block for other important molecules like nucleotides, glycoproteins, and glycolipids. Glucose is primarily found in two forms in the body:

A. Blood Glucose: This is also known as blood sugar, and it is the glucose that is circulating in the blood. To maintain a balance between glucose availability and energy requirements, the body tightly regulates blood glucose levels.

B. Glucose in storage: Glycogen, a complex carbohydrate composed of glucose molecules, is the form of glucose that is stored in the liver and muscles. The liver and muscles can convert glycogen into glucose and release it into the bloodstream as a quick energy source when energy requirements rise.

Why Glucose Is So Important In Our Diet

Because the body uses glucose as its primary source of energy, it is essential to include glucose in our diet. Our digestive systems break down carbohydrates into glucose molecules when we consume grains, dairy products, fruits, and vegetables. After that, glucose enters the circulation and is used to produce energy.

In addition to providing energy, glucose is necessary for the brain and other organs to function properly. For instance, the brain gets almost all of its energy from glucose. Fatigue, dizziness, and difficulty concentrating are all signs that the body doesn't get enough glucose from the diet.

However, it is essential to keep in mind that not all glucose sources are created equal. Simple sugars, which are found in candy, soda, and other sweetened beverages, can quickly raise and lower blood sugar levels, which can be bad for your health over time. It's smarter to get glucose from complex carbs like entire grains, natural products, and vegetables, which give a consistent, supported wellspring of energy and contain other significant supplements like fiber, nutrients, and minerals.

Since glucose is a nutrient that the body needs, it's important to keep blood glucose levels stable for good health. Some of the glucose's most important functions are as follows:

A. Production of energy: Cells get most of their energy from glucose through a process known as cellular respiration where glucose is broken down into energy. This energy is eventually used to power a variety of bodily functions like muscle contraction, brain activity, and the creation of new cells and tissues.

B. Cognitive function: For the brain to function properly, glucose is very important. The brain would be unable to perform essential functions like thinking, learning, and memory without glucose.

C. Storage: The body stores glucose in the liver and muscles as glycogen. To maintain normal blood sugar levels, the liver can release stored glycogen into the bloodstream when blood glucose levels drop.

D. Controlling blood sugar levels: Blood sugar levels are crucially regulated by glucose. Insulin, which is produced by the pancreas, enables glucose to enter cells for use as fuel or saved for later. This helps keep blood sugar levels in check.

Generally, glucose is a basic supplement that is fundamental for the majority of physical processes, including energy creation, and cerebrum capability.

Glucose Spikes can be Dangerous for our Health: Here's Why

The term "glucose spikes" refers to an abrupt and significant rise in blood glucose levels. Fast absorption of certain food into the bloodstream results in a sudden increase in glucose levels which creates an excess of insulin for storage or use as fuel. However, if an excessive amount of insulin is produced, it may result in a drop in blood sugar, which may cause feelings of hunger, irritability, and fatigue.

Glucose spikes are frequently caused by foods and beverages high in simple sugars, such as candy, soda, and other sweetened beverages. White bread, white rice, and pasta are examples of processed and refined carbohydrates that can increase blood glucose levels.

Over time, glucose surges can be harmful to your health because they increase exposure to inflammation, heart disease, insulin resistance, type 2 diabetes, and weight gain. It is crucial to choose healthy forms of carbohydrates like whole grains, fruits, and veggies to support the maintenance of steady blood sugar levels and enhance general health.

Glucose spikes can be destructive to well-being since they can prompt a few adverse consequences on the body. Glucose spikes can be harmful for several reasons, including the following:

A. Insulin sensitivity: The body makes insulin to help bring glucose into cells for energy or storage when blood glucose levels rise. However, insulin resistance, which occurs when cells become less responsive to insulin, can occur if glucose levels remain consistently high. The likelihood of developing type 2 diabetes may rise as a result.

B. Inflammation: High blood sugar levels can create inflammation in the body, which can hasten the development of persistent conditions like cancer, heart disease, and Alzheimer's disease.

C. Gaining weight: Sugary snacks and beverages, which spike blood glucose levels, can make you gain weight over time. This is because these food sources will generally be high in calories and can add to gorging.

D. Risk factors for metabolic syndrome: Glucose surges may contribute to the development of metabolic syndrome, which is characterized by high blood pressure, high blood sugar, excess body fat around the waist, and abnormal cholesterol levels. People with metabolic syndrome are more likely to develop heart disease, stroke, and type 2 diabetes.

Effects of these Sugar Spikes on our Health

There are many unpleasant short-term symptoms associated with spikes and dips, and they differ from person to person. For some, they include dizziness, nausea, heart palpitations, sweats, food cravings, and stress. For others, they include exhaustion and brain fog. For many, a glucose spike can also result in poor mood or anxiety.

SHORT-TERM EFFECTS

A. Constant hunger: If you feel famished again soon after eating, glucose is to blame. When contrasting two meals with the same amount of calories, the one that causes a less dramatic rise in blood sugar levels will keep you fuller for longer. Second, an elevated insulin level is a sign of persistent hunger. Our hormones become confused when our bodies have an excessive amount of insulin that has accumulated over many years of glucose surges. The signal from the hormone leptin, which alerts us when we are replete and should stop eating, is blocked, and ghrelin, which alerts us when we are hungry, takes over.

B. Cravings: Even a tiny drop in glucose levels causes us to crave high-calorie foods. Our glucose levels are constantly falling, particularly after every spike, which is a problem. And the crash will be more severe the greater the spike has been. That's excellent news because it shows that insulin is working as intended and storing extra glucose in a variety of compartments. However, it also implies that we suddenly have a craving for a cookie, a burger, or both.

C. Chronic fatigue: When the mitochondria are overloaded with glucose, energy synthesis is hampered, and we become fatigued. Usually, individuals born with mitochondrial defects are only able to exercise for half as long as people who are otherwise healthy. Picking up your child from school is more difficult, carrying groceries is exhausting, and you won't be able to manage stress as well as you once could if you have damaged mitochondria. To surmount difficult situations, both physically and mentally, mitochondria must produce energy. When we consume something sweet, we may believe that we are giving our bodies the energy they need, but this is merely an illusion brought on by the dopamine surge in our brains that gives us a high. Every spike reduces our mitochondria's capacity over the long run.

D. Poor sleep: The sudden awakening in the middle of the night with a racing pulse is a common sign of dysregulated glucose. Sleep apnea in males and insomnia in postmenopausal women are both linked to elevated glucose levels or the immediate aftermath of a significant glucose spike. Flatten your curves if you want a restful night's slumber.

E. Colds and coronavirus complications: Your immune system becomes briefly compromised after a glucose spike. You can say goodbye to five-star immune defenses against invaders if your blood sugar levels are consistently high. You will also be more prone to infection, which comes out to be true for the coronavirus in particular.

F. Worsens Menopause: Menopause causes drastic drops in hormone levels, which can feel like an earthquake. As a result, women may experience symptoms such as decreased libido, night sweats, insomnia, and more. Menopause is made worse by elevated or unstable insulin and glucose levels. However, there is a promise because flattening glucose curves is linked to a reduction in menopause symptoms like insomnia.

G. Migraine: Even though this area of research is still in its infancy, statistics show that women who have insulin resistance are twice as likely as women who do not experience frequent migraine headaches. Things appear to improve when insulin levels in sufferers are lowered

H. Memory and cognitive function issues: Be careful what you eat right before a test, when you balance your checkbook, or when you initiate an argument that you want to win. When you need an energy boost, it's simple to grab something sweet, but this decision may impair your cognitive function. It turns out that memory and cognitive performance can be affected by significant glucose spikes. After fasting all night, this impact is at its worst first thing in the morning.

LONG-TERM EFFECTS

I. Acne and other skin conditions: Consuming foods that are starchy and sweet can start a chain reaction that can cause acne on your face and body and even make your skin appear noticeably redder. This is because many skin diseases, such as eczema and psoriasis, are fueled by inflammation, which, as you learned, is a result of high blood sugar levels. Acne, zits, and inflammation all subside when we eat in a manner that flattens our glucose curves.

J. Aging and arthritis: You may have spiked your glucose tens of thousands of times, depending on your diet. This will have an impact not only on your external appearance but also on your internal age. The faster we age, the more frequently we spike. Aging refers to the gradual deterioration of our cells caused by glycation, free radicals, and subsequent inflammation. Free radicals likewise harm collagen, the protein which causes drooping skin and wrinkles and can prompt irritation in joints, rheumatoid joint pain, corruption of ligaments, and osteoarthritis: Our joints hurt, our bones become brittle, and we absolutely cannot run in the park.

K. Alzheimer's and dementia: Of all organs, the mind utilizes the most energy. There are a lot of mitochondria there. This indicates that our brain is susceptible to the effects of excess glucose in our bodies. Like all other cells, neurons in our brain experience oxidative stress: Because they increase oxidative stress, repeated glucose spikes cause neuroinflammation and eventually cognitive dysfunction. In addition, almost all chronic degenerative diseases, including Alzheimer's, are exacerbated by chronic inflammation. Indeed, the relationship between Alzheimer's disease and glucose levels is so strong that the condition is sometimes referred to as "type 3 diabetes" or "diabetes of the brain." For instance, people who have type 2 diabetes are four times more likely than people who don't have diabetes to get Alzheimer's disease. The signs are also evident early on: Memory and learning problems are linked to poorly controlled glucose levels in type 2 diabetics. However, when patients follow a glucose-stabilizing diet, they can experience both short-term and long-term improvements in their memory and cognition.

L. Cancer risk: One in two children born today will acquire cancer at some point in their lives. Additionally, smoking and poor nutrition are the primary causes of 50% of cancers. To start, studies suggest that DNA mutations caused by free radicals may be the origin of cancer. Second, inflammation encourages the growth of malignancy. Finally, cancer spreads even more quickly when there is more insulin present. The data demonstrate that glucose is essential to many of these processes: prediabetic individuals, whose fasting glucose levels are greater than 100 mg/dL, have a more than twofold increased risk of dying from cancer. Thus, a crucial stage in assisting in the development of cancer prevention is the flattening of the glucose and insulin curves.

M. Depressive episodes: Since your brain lacks sensory nerves, it cannot warn you of a problem by producing discomfort as other organs can. You experience emotional disturbances instead, such as low mood. People who consume a diet that causes fluctuating blood sugar levels experience worsening moods, an increase in depressive symptoms, and more mood disturbances than those who consume a diet with a comparable nutritional profile but with stable blood sugar levels. Any attempt to mildly flatten the curve could help you feel better because the symptoms worsen as the spikes become more extreme.

N. Gut issues: It's in our stomach that our food is separated into atoms, retained in our blood, or conveyed to waste disposal. Therefore, it should come as no surprise that diet is linked to bowel distress, such as the leaky gut, irritable bowel syndrome, and slowed intestinal transit. The connection between spikes in glucose levels and particular digestive issues is still up for debate, but it appears that high glucose levels may increase leaky gut syndrome. Food allergies and additional autoimmune diseases like Crohn's disease and rheumatoid arthritis follow. Thankfully, adopting a glucose-flattening diet can quickly alleviate acid reflux or heartburn, sometimes within a day.

O. Heart disease: Cholesterol frequently takes center stage when we discuss heart disease. However, the conversation is changing since "too much cholesterol" is not the only factor. We now know that inflammation and a particular type of cholesterol (LDL pattern B) cause heart disease. This is the case for a reason, according to scientists. It is linked to insulin, fructose, and glucose. For fructose and glucose, it is important to note that the lining of our blood vessels is made of cells, and these cells are particularly susceptible to mitochondrial stress, which results in oxidative stress when glucose and fructose spike. These cells suffer as a result and the linings become bumpy, making it easier for fat particles to stick to the uneven surface. For insulin, our liver starts producing LDL pattern B, a small, dense type of cholesterol that creeps along the edges of the vessels, where it is likely to get caught when insulin levels are too high. If and when that cholesterol is oxidized — it lodges under the coating of our veins and sticks there. Plaque develops and discourages the stream, and this is the way coronary illness begins. Spikes drive these three cycles. Flattening our insulin, glucose, and fructose curves would be beneficial to our hearts.

Insulin and Hyperinsulinism: let's Have a Look

The pancreas produces the hormone insulin, which is essential for preserving the body's normal blood sugar levels. To tell cells to take glucose from the bloodstream and either use it for energy or store it for later use, the pancreas releases insulin when blood sugar levels increase after a meal.

There are several reasons why hyperinsulinism, or high blood insulin levels, can be harmful to health. The following are some of the negative effects of hyperinsulinism:

1. Insulin sensitivity: Over the long haul, elevated degrees of insulin in the blood can prompt insulin obstruction, a condition in which cells become less receptive to insulin. As a consequence, type 2 diabetes risk is raised and blood sugar levels are higher making it harder for cells to absorb glucose from the bloodstream.

2. Inflammation: High insulin levels can exacerbate inflammation in the body, which increases the chance of chronic illnesses like heart disease, cancer, and Alzheimer's disease.

3.Gaining weight: The body's regulation of fat storage also involves insulin. Insulin levels that are too high can encourage fat storage, which can lead to weight gain and an increased risk of obesity.

4. Unbalanced hormones: The hormone insulin interacts with estrogen, testosterone, and cortisol, among other hormones, in the body. High insulin levels can upset the equilibrium of these chemicals, prompting a scope of medical problems.

5. Risk factors for metabolic syndrome: Metabolic syndrome, a cluster of diseases that also includes high blood pressure, high blood sugar, extra body fat, and abnormal cholesterol levels, frequently contains hyperinsulinism. People with metabolic syndrome are more prone to develop heart disease, stroke, and type 2 diabetes.

In summary, hyperinsulinism can be destructive to well-being since it can add to insulin opposition, aggravation, weight gain, hormonal uneven characters, and an expanded gamble of metabolic condition. To aid in the prevention of hyperinsulinism and the risks it poses to one's health, it is essential to maintain healthy blood sugar levels through a well-balanced diet, regular exercise, and other healthy ways of living.

Correlation between Blood sugar and Hunger Hormones

Ghrelin and leptin, two hormones that control hunger and satiety, are greatly influenced by blood sugar levels.

1. Ghrelin: This is a hormone made by the stomach that makes you want to eat more and makes you eat more. Ghrelin levels tend to rise when blood sugar levels are low, which can make you feel hungry and want to eat.

2. Leptin: This hormone is made by the fat cells make and it helps the body balance its energy supply by reducing appetite and increasing energy expenditure. At the point when glucose levels are high, leptin levels will generally build, which signals to the body that it has sufficient energy and diminish sensations of appetite. There are instances in which these hormonal mechanisms may become out of balance, resulting in unbalanced hunger and satiety. For instance, the body's ability to respond to leptin can be hindered by insulin resistance, resulting in persistent hunger and overeating. Additionally, consuming sugary snacks and beverages, as well as other foods that cause rapid spikes in blood sugar, can cause the release of a significant amount of insulin, which in turn can result in a drop in blood sugar levels and feelings of hunger.

Maintaining stable glucose levels through a fair eating routine, regular exercise, and other sound ways of life propensities can assist with controlling hunger hormones. It is important to avoid consuming sugary snacks and beverages, as well as other foods that can cause rapid spikes in blood sugar, and subsequently cause the release of a significant amount of insulin, which in turn can result in a drop in blood sugar levels and feelings of hunger.

Flattening your Glucose Curves: Here's How

A glucose curve refers to the pattern of changes in blood glucose levels over time. The type and quantity of carbohydrates consumed, physical activity, stress, and overall health can all have an impact on glucose curves. Blood glucose levels typically stay within a narrow range throughout the day in healthy individuals, with only minor changes caused by food or activity.

However, glucose curves can be more erratic, with significant spikes and dips in blood sugar levels, in people who have diabetes or other health issues related to blood sugar. This may lead to several health problems, such as a higher chance of heart disease, kidney damage, nerve damage, and eye problems. Changing one's lifestyle to support steady blood sugar levels and regularly checking one's blood glucose levels can help lower the risk of these health issues and enhance one's general health and well-being. To help you flatten your glucose curves, here are some solutions:

A. Maintain a healthy diet: Eating a varied diet with a variety of complex carbs, protein, and healthy fats can help to delay the uptake of glucose into the bloodstream. This lessens the chance of blood sugar surges.

B. Avoid processed and sugary foods: Foods rich in sugar and refined carbs can quickly raise blood sugar levels, followed by crashes that can leave you feeling famished and exhausted. Keep your glucose curves stable by limiting your intake of these foods.

C. Regular exercise: Your body's ability to use glucose more effectively and to maintain stable blood sugar levels can be aided by increasing insulin sensitivity through regular exercise.

D. Keep hydrated: Drinking a lot of water can flush out excess sugar from your bloodstream and subsequently prevent dehydration, which can lead to spikes in blood sugar,

E. Get sufficient sleep: Sleep is important for controlling blood sugar levels, so getting enough good sleep every night is important for keeping glucose curves stable.

Eliminating Added Sugars

During processing or preparation, any type of sugar or sweetener that is added to meals and drinks is referred to as added sugar. Contrary to the sugars found naturally in fruits and veggies, added sugars are not necessary for a healthy diet and, when eaten in excess, can lead to several health problems. The following list of typical additional carbohydrates includes:

A. Corn syrup high in fructose: This liquid sweetener, which is produced from maize starch, is commonly used in processed meals and drinks.
B. Regular sugar: Table sugar, also known as sucrose, is a crystalline product made from sugar cane or sugar beets.
C. Dark sugar: This molasses-infused sugar is created by mixing purified white sugar with molasses.
D. Powdered sugar or confectioner's sugar: This is finely ground white sugar blended in with a limited quantity of cornstarch.
E. Honey: Honey is a sweet and viscous liquid made by bees from flower nectar.
F. Maple syrup: A sweet, tacky syrup produced using the sap of maple trees.
G. Molasses: a dark, thick syrup produced as a byproduct of sugar production.
H. Agave nectar: A characteristic sugar got from the agave plant.
I. Concentrated juice of fruits: a concentrated form of fruit juice that is frequently added to processed foods as a sweetener.

While small amounts of added sugars can be a part of a healthy diet, it's essential to remember that excessive added sugar intake has been related to obesity, diabetes, and heart disease. It is advised to consume as little extra sugar as feasible. Men and women should each drink no more than 6 and no more than 9 tablespoons of added sugar, respectively, each day.

Keep in mind that not all carbohydrates are made equally. Fructose, for instance, may have a greater impact on your metabolism than other sugars, even though all additional sugars can be harmful to your health if you consume too much of them. As a result, it's critical to limit your intake of added sugars and put whole, unprocessed foods first in your diet.

Making Better Low-Sugar Choices

Wiping out added sugars from your eating regimen can be a difficult but remunerating process. To help you get started, here are some suggestions:

A. Reduce the intake of processed foods: Since processed foods typically contain a lot of added sugars, reducing your intake of these foods can help you reduce your intake as a whole. Choose whole, unprocessed meals instead, such as fruits, veggies, whole grains, lean proteins, and healthful lipids.

B. Read food labels: Begin by perusing food names and fixing records cautiously to recognize wellsprings of added sugars. Corn syrup, dextrose, fructose, glucose, sucrose, and maltose are examples of words to look for.

C. Avoid Drinks with sugar: Sweet beverages like pop, squeeze, and sports drinks are probably the greatest wellsprings of added sugars in an eating regimen. Change to water, or unsweetened tea.

D. Choose sweeteners made from nature: Stevia, monk fruit extract, or raw honey are all-natural sweeteners that can be used in moderation if necessary.

E. Homemade meals: You can control the ingredients and avoid the added sugars that can be found in restaurant meals and packaged foods by cooking at home.

F. Be aware of toppings and sauces: Numerous toppings and sauces, for example, ketchup, grill sauce, and salad dressings, can be high in added sugars. Make your own at home or look for alternatives with less sugar.

G. Reduce your intake gradually: It can be difficult to eliminate added sugars at once, so reduce your intake gradually over time to ease the transition.

Keep in mind that moderation and balance are the keys to a healthy diet. Even though cutting out added sugars can be good for your health as a whole, it's important to have treats and other indulgences in moderation.

Here's what Sugar Detox Will Do For Your Health

Sugar detox is a dietary methodology that includes dispensing with or radically diminishing the use of added sugars from one's eating routine for a predetermined period. A sugar detox aims to help people break free of their sugar addiction, lessen their reliance on sweet foods, and improve their overall health.

The majority of highly processed and packaged foods, soft drinks, candies, baked goods, and other sugary snacks contain added sugars. Several health problems, such as obesity, type 2 diabetes, heart disease, and even some types of cancer, have been related to an excessive intake of added sugars. Additionally, these foods frequently lack essential nutrients and are high in calories.

In a sugar detox, the diet is changed to include whole, unprocessed foods such as fruits, veggies, lean proteins, and healthful fats. This modification to one's diet has the potential to support the stabilization of blood sugar levels, lessen body inflammation, and raise one's level of overall energy and well-being.

Depending on the goals and requirements of the individual, the duration of a sugar detox may vary. Certain individuals might decide to do a momentary detox for a couple of days or seven days, while others might settle on a more extended-term approach enduring a little while or even months.

It's important to remember that a sugar detox should be done with the help of a trained medical professional, especially for people who already have health problems. Moreover, in the wake of finishing a sugar detox, it's vital to keep a fair eating routine that incorporates moderate measures of regular sugars from sources like leafy foods items to guarantee sufficient supplement consumption. A sugar detox might be chosen for one of the following reasons:

A. Overall Better Health: Too much sugar can cause several issues, including diabetes, dental issues, obesity, and heart disease. Sugar reduction can help lower these conditions' risk and improve overall health.

B. Heightened Levels Of Energy: When consumed in large quantities, sugar can result in energy crashes and fatigue. A sugar detox can help keep blood sugar levels in check, giving you more energy for the whole day.

C. Better Emotional Wellness: A diet high in sugar may contribute to depression and anxiety, according to some research. Sugar reduction can help improve mood and reduce anxiety and depression symptoms.

D. Shedding Pounds: Sugar has a lot of calories and can make you gain weight. Sugar reduction can assist in calorie reduction and weight loss.

E. Healthier Complexion: Sugar can cause inflammation in the body, which can cause acne and premature aging of the skin. Sugar consumption can benefit skin health.

In general, a sugar detox can be beneficial for enhancing one's health and well-being. However, it is essential to keep in mind that, when consumed in moderation, sugar is still an important source of energy and nutrients, and that eliminating it may not be necessary or sustainable for all individuals. Before making any major changes to your diet, consult a doctor or other medical professional.

Start by Detoxing the Kitchen!

This is your opportunity to start a revolt and clear out the barriers to your health and weight loss so that you can make your kitchen a real haven of nourishment and healing. Clean out your refrigerator, cabinets, and storage of any item that fits one of the following groups:

i. Anything produced in a factory and packaged-Unless it's a whole food that's canned, like sardines or artichokes, and only contains a few real ingredients, like water or salt, it's not real food.

ii. Sugar-sweetened beverages and fruit juices, as well as honey, molasses, agave, maple syrup, organic cane juice, and artificial sweeteners.

iii. Anything made with refined veggie oils or hydrogenated oils like corn or soybean oil.

iv. Anything that has a label or has been processed in any way and contains artificial sweeteners, preservatives, additives, coloring, or dyes

v. The following items must also be eliminated; however, if you are hesitant to do so, simply conceal them from view during the detox as long as you believe you can safely avoid them:

vi. Everything is made with gluten, like bread, pasta, bagels, and so on.

vii. All grains, including those without gluten.

viii. All dairy products, including yogurt, cheese, and milk.

SUGAR-DETOX GROCERY LIST

VEGETABLES

- ✓ Peppers
- ✓ Onions
- ✓ Zucchini
- ✓ Broccoli
- ✓ Frozen spinach
- ✓ Frozen Peas
- ✓ Carrots
- ✓ Cabbage
- ✓ Romaine
- ✓ Tomatoes
- ✓ Lettuce
- ✓ Garlic Peas
- ✓ Potatoes
- ✓ Pumpkin
- ✓ Squash
- ✓ Mushrooms
- ✓ Eggplant
- ✓ Cauliflower
- ✓ Cucumbers
- ✓ Celery leaves
- ✓ Spinach
- ✓ Green beans

FRUIT

- ✓ Oranges
- ✓ Tangerines
- ✓ Lemons
- ✓ Apples
- ✓ Pears
- ✓ Avocado
- ✓ Banana
- ✓ Grapefruit
- ✓ Berries
- ✓ Peaches

DAIRY

- ✓ Greek Yogurt
- ✓ Romano cheese
- ✓ Reduced Fat Ricotta
- ✓ Parmesan
- ✓ Fresh Mozzarella

NON DAIRY

- ✓ Soy milk
- ✓ Coconut milk

MEAT AND POULTRY

- ✓ Chicken
- ✓ Eggs
- ✓ Turkey

FISH AND SEAFOOD

- ✓ Cod
- ✓ Shrimp
- ✓ Tilapia
- ✓ Salmon
- ✓ Halibut
- ✓ Sea bass

GRAINS AND BREAD

- ✓ Whole grain bread
- ✓ Breadcrumbs
- ✓ Whole wheat pasta shells
- ✓ Crushed freekeh
- ✓ Quinoa
- ✓ Barley

BEANS

- ✓ Lentils
- ✓ Red kidney beans
- ✓ Bean sprouts
- ✓ White beans
- ✓ Chickpeas
- ✓ Yellow Split Pea

FATS, SEEDS & NUTS

- ✓ Chia Seeds
- ✓ Extra-Virgin Olive Oil
- ✓ Almond flour
- ✓ Almonds
- ✓ Walnuts
- ✓ Pine Nuts
- ✓ Chestnut Flour
- ✓ Sunflower seeds
- ✓ Hemp Hearts
- ✓ Pumpkin seeds
- ✓ Squash seeds
- ✓ Flax Seed

PANTRY

- ✓ Low-sodium diced tomatoes
- ✓ Tomato Paste
- ✓ Olives
- ✓ Sundried Tomatoes
- ✓ Capers
- ✓ Balsamic vinegar
- ✓ Honey
- ✓ Stevia

HERBS AND SPICES

- ✓ Oregano
- ✓ Turmeric
- ✓ Parsley
- ✓ Basil
- ✓ Cumin
- ✓ Paprika
- ✓ Cinnamon
- ✓ Nutmeg
- ✓ Pepper/low-sodium salt

30-DAY MEAL PLAN

Day	BREAKFAST	LUNCH	DINNER	SNACK/DESSERT
WEEK 1				
1	Asparagus and Soy milk Omelet	Beef and Vegetable Soup	Mushrooms & spinach	Gingered Pecans
2	Watercress Cranberry Smoothie	Turkey Bacon and Broccoli Salad	Broad Bean Salad with Turmeric Potatoes	Sugar-Free Chocolate Mousse
3	Sugar-Free Granola	Chickpea salad	Low-Sugar Shrimp Scampi & Squash	Fried Queso Blanco
4	Seedy Breakfast	Tomato and basil salad	Lamb and Lentil Stew	Sweet Potato Chips
5	Grape Berry Smoothie	Loaded Greens and Seeds	Grilled Chicken with Avocado Salsa	Sugar-Free Chocolate Banana Ice Cream
6	Walnut and almond porridge	Citrus Poached Salmon	Aubergine, Potato & Chickpea	Sugar-Free Spinach Brownies
7	Apple, beet, and strawberry smoothie	Cucumber and Sprouts	Slow Cooker Pulled Pork	Roasted Pine Nuts
WEEK 2				
8	Oatmeal with coconut milk	Broccoli Cauliflower Fry	Turkey and Vegetable Stir Fry	Tofu Lemon Pie
9	Scrambled eggs with salmon	Basil Turkey with Roasted Tomatoes	Cheesy Lemon Quinoa Salad	Sugar-Free Chocolate Mousse
10	Ginger pancakes	Tofu and Spinach Lasagne	Grilled Chicken with Avocado Salsa	Veggie Sticks with Hummus
11	Avocado and Tomato Breakfast	Spinach and Walnut Salad	Lemon Garlic Chicken	Sweet Potato Chips
12	Asparagus and Soy milk Omelet	Citrus Poached Salmon	Stir-Fried Vegetables & Rice	Stacked Carrot & Courgette

13	Tofu & Tomato Breakfast	Bacon, Leek, Thyme Farro	Spicy Lamb and Veggie Skewers	Tofu Lemon Pie
14	Fiber-loaded muesli	Tomato and basil salad	Turkey and Vegetable Stir Fry	Fried Queso Blanco
WEEK 3				
15	Asparagus and Soy milk Omelet	Tomato & Cauliflower Spaghetti	Chicken and Vegetable Stir-Fry	Roasted Pine Nuts
16	Walnut porridge	Coconut Ground Beef	Low-Sugar Tuna Salad	Veggie Sticks with Hummus
17	Grape Berry Smoothie	Low-Sugar Asparagus Salad	Lamb Chops with Herb Rub	Sugar-Free Chocolate Banana Ice Cream
18	Oatmeal with coconut milk	Slow Cooker Pulled Pork	Olive and Kale Salad	Gingered Pecans
19	Omelet with mushrooms and peppers	Salmon in Pesto	Tomato & Basil Gazpacho	Stacked Carrot & Courgette
20	Cherry and kale smoothie	Tomato & Avocado Warmer	No-Sugar Ginger Beef and Broccoli	Sugar-Free Spinach Brownies
21	Scrambled eggs with salmon	Mushrooms & spinach	Chicken and Vegetable Stir-Fry	Sugar-Free Chocolate Mousse
WEEK 4				
22	Watercress Cranberry Smoothie	Roasted Lemon Herb Chicken	Coral lentil & Swiss chard soup	Sugar-Free Chocolate Mousse
23	Low Sugar Overnight Oats	Carrot, Spinach & Almond Salad	Swiss Chard & Haddock	Roasted Pine Nuts
24	Avocado and Tomato Breakfast	Spinach and Walnut Salad	Crusted Salmon with dill	Fried Queso Blanco
25	Tofu & Tomato Breakfast	Mango, Jalapeño & bean salad	Creamy Baked Chicken	Sugar-Free Spinach Brownies
26	Omelet with mushrooms and peppers	Beef Mushroom Yakisoba	Lentils and Zucchini	Low-sugar Cod Ceviche
27	Spicy South-western Breakfast Bowl	Tomato & Cauliflower Spaghetti	Lamb with peas	Tofu Lemon Pie

28	Seedy Breakfast	Beef and Mushroom Lettuce Wraps	Carrot, Spinach & Almond Salad	Veggie Sticks with Hummus
WEEK 5				
29	Walnut porridge	Lentil & Butternut Squash Stew	Ground Pork Stir Fry	Stacked Carrot & Courgette
30	Low Sugar Overnight Oats	Low-Sugar Power Salad	Coconut Ground Beef	Gingered Pecans

MEASUREMENT CONVERSION CHART

TO CONVERT X » Y	1 OF THIS	EQUALS THIS
VOLUME TO WEIGHT		
tablespoons » teaspoons	1 tablespoon	3 teaspoons
tablespoons » ounces	1 tablespoon	0.5 ounces
tablespoons » sticks of butter	1 tablespoon	0.125 sticks of butter
tablespoons » cups	1 tablespoon	0.0625 cups
teaspoons » tablespoons	1 teaspoon	0.33 tablespoons
teaspoons » cups	1 teaspoon	0.02 cups
teaspoons » ounces	1 teaspoon	0.16 ounces
ounces » tablespoons	1 fluid ounce	2 tablespoons
ounces » teaspoons	1 fluid ounce	6 teaspoons
ounces » cups	1 fluid ounce	0.125 cups
cups » ounces	1 cup	8 ounces
cups » tablespoons	1 cup	16 tablespoons
cups » teaspoons	1 cup	48 teaspoons
cups » pints	1 cup	0.5 pints
cups » quarts	1 cup	0.25 quarts
cups » gallons	1 cup	0.0625 gallons
pints » cups	1 pint	2 cups
quarts » pints	1 quart	2 pints
quarts » cups	1 quart	4 cups
gallon » quarts	1 gallon	4 quarts
gallon » cups	1 gallon	16 cups
pinch » teaspoons	1 pinch	0.1 teaspoons
dash » teaspoons	1 dash	0.2 teaspoons
cup dry beans » pounds	1 cup dry beans	0.4 pounds
cup butter » pounds	1 cup butter	0.5 pounds
cup choc. chips » ounces	1 cup chocolate chips	6 ounces
cup cheerios » ounces	1 cup cheerios	1.33 ounces
cup cocoa » ounces	1 cup cocoa	3 ounces
cup corn syrup » ounces	1 cup corn syrup	11.5 ounces
cup cornmeal » ounces	1 cup cornmeal	4.5 ounces
cup flour » ounces	1 cup flour	4 ounces
cup flour » pounds	1 cup flour	0.25 pounds
cup honey » pounds	1 cup honey	0.75 pounds
cup honey » ounces	1 cup honey	12 ounces

cup jam » ounces	1 cup jam	12 ounces
cup molasses » ounces	1 cup molasses	11.6 ounces
cup oats » ounces	1 cup oats	3.5 ounces
cup oats » pounds	1 cup oats	0.22 pounds
cup oil » ounces	1 cup oil	7.5 ounces
cup peanut butter » ounces	1 cup peanut butter	9.5 ounces
cup raisins » ounces	1 cup raisins	5.5 ounces
cup rice » ounces	1 cup rice	7 ounces
cup rice » pounds	1 cup rice	0.4375 pounds
cup rice flour » ounces	1 cup rice flour	4.5 ounces
cup shortening » ounces	1 cup shortening	7 ounces
cup sour cream » ounces	1 cup sour cream	8 ounces
cup sugar » ounces	1 cup sugar	7 ounces
cup sugar » pounds	1 cup sugar	0.4375 pounds
cup sugar (brown) » ounces	1 cup brown sugar	7.5 ounces
cup sugar (powdered) » ounces	1 cup powdered sugar	4 ounces
cup water » ounces	1 cup water	8.3 ounces
cup walnuts (chopped) » ounces	1 cup walnuts	4.3 ounces
cup wheat » pounds	1 cup wheat	0.48 pounds
cup dried milk (nonfat) » ounces	1 cup dried milk (nonfat)	3 ounces
egg (powdered) » ounces	1 egg (powdered)	0.5 ounces
egg (large) » ounces	1 egg (large)	2 ounces
egg white » teaspoons	1 egg white	8 teaspoons
egg white » cups	1 egg white	48 cups
egg yolk » teaspoons	1 egg yolk	4 teaspoons
stick butter » cups	1 stick butter	0.5 cups
stick butter » ounces	1 stick butter	4 ounces
stick butter » tablespoons	1 stick butter	8 tablespoons
tablespoons baking soda » ounces	1 tablespoon baking soda	0.5 ounces
tablespoons baking powder » ounces	1 tablespoon baking powder	0.5 ounces
tablespoons baking powder » pounds	1 tablespoon baking powder	0.03125 pounds
tablespoons cocoa » ounces	1 tablespoon cocoa	0.1875 ounces
tablespoons cocoa » pounds	1 tablespoon cocoa	0.01 pounds
tablespoons cornstarch » ounces	1 tablespoon cornstarch	0.33 ounces
tablespoons jam » ounces	1 tablespoon jam	0.75 ounces
tablespoons honey » ounces	1 tablespoon honey	0.75 ounces
tablespoons honey » pounds	1 tablespoon honey	0.0468 pounds
tablespoons oil » ounces	1 tablespoon oil	0.46875 ounces
tablespoons peanut butter » ounces	1 tablespoon peanut butter	0.59375 ounces

tablespoons salt » ounces	1 tablespoon salt	0.6 ounces
tablespoons shortening » ounces	1 tablespoon shortening	0.4375 ounces
tablespoons spices » ounces	1 tablespoon spices	0.25 ounces
tablespoons vinegar » ounces	1 tablespoon vinegar	0.5 ounces
tablespoons yeast » ounces	1 tablespoon yeast	0.5 ounces
tablespoons yeast » ounces	1 tablespoon yeast	0.33 ounces
teaspoons baking soda » ounces	1 teaspoon baking soda	0.16 ounces
teaspoons baking powder » ounces	1 teaspoon baking powder	0.16 ounces
teaspoons salt » ounces	1 teaspoon salt	0.2 ounces
pound flour » cups	1 pound flour	4 cups
pound sugar » cups	1 pound sugar	2.285 cups
ounces oats » cups	1-ounce oats	0.285 cups
Pound rice » cups	1 pound rice	2.285 cups
ounces salt » teaspoons	1-ounce salt	5 teaspoons
ounces jam » tablespoons	1-ounce jam	1.33 tablespoons
MASS TO WEIGHT		
ounce » pounds	1 ounce	0.0625 pounds
ounce » grams	1 ounce	28.35 grams
pounds » ounces	1 pound	16 ounces
pounds » kg	1 pound	0.45kg
kg » pounds	1 kg	2.2 pounds
grams » ounces	1 gram	0.035ounces
ENGLISH TO METRIC		
cup (U.S.) » mL	1 cup (U.S.)	236.58 mL
cup (U.K.) » mL	1 cup (U.K.)	284 mL
cup (Australia) » mL	1 cup (Australia)	250 mL
gallon (US) » L	1 gallon (US)	3.785 L
quart (US) » L	1 quart (US)	0.946 L
pint (US) » L	1 pint (US)	0.47 L
ounces (US) » mL	1 fluid ounce (US)	29.57mL
tablespoons (US) » mL	1 tablespoon (US)	14.78 mL
teaspoons (US) » mL	1 teaspoon (US)	4.9285 mL
mL » cc	1 mL	1 cc

Low Sugar Overnight Oats

Makes: 4-6

NUTRITION: Calories: 190|Carbohydrates: 28g|Protein: 7g|Fat: 5g |Saturated Fat: 1g|Fiber: 6g|Sugar: 1g

INGREDIENTS:

- ½ teaspoon kosher salt
- 1½ cups steel-cut oats
- 1½ teaspoons ground cinnamon
- vanilla extract, 1 teaspoon
- 4 cups water
- ground flaxseed meal, 3 tablespoons
- 2 mashed ripe bananas
- ½ teaspoon freshly grated nutmeg
- 2 cups milk

INSTRUCTIONS:

a) Mix all the ingredients in the bottom of a 4- to 6-quart Crockpot.
b) Cook on medium for about 7½ hours.

Fiber-loaded muesli

Makes: 1

NUTRITION: Calories: 324 | Fat: 12.1 g |Carbohydrate: 51 g
|Protein: 10.2 g|Sugar: 1g

INGREDIENTS:

• rolled oats, 2 cups
• whole-wheat bran flakes, 2 cups
• unsweetened, dried cranberries, 1 cup
• hulled sunflower seeds, ¼ cup

• chopped walnuts, sliced and unsalted, ¼ cup
• Skim milk or fat-free yogurt to serve

INSTRUCTIONS:

a) Combine everything in a bowl or a storage bag.
b) Stir everything together.

Walnut porridge

Makes: 4

NUTRITION: Calories: 292 | Fat: 7.5g | Carbohydrates: 9.6g
| Sugars: 1.2g | Protein: 8g

INGREDIENTS:

• ½ cup pecans
• unsweetened almond milk, 4 cups
• ½ cup almonds
• sunflower seeds, ¼ cup
• chia seeds, ¼ cup

• unsweetened coconut flakes, ¼ cup
• ginger powder, ¼ teaspoon
• cinnamon powder, ½ teaspoon
• powdered stevia, 1 teaspoon
• almond butter, 1 tablespoon

INSTRUCTIONS:

a) Use a food blender to combine walnuts, almonds, and sunflower seeds.
b) Combine the nut mixture with the chia seeds, coconut flakes, almond milk, seasonings, and stevia in a pan.
c) Bring to a moderate boil, then reduce the heat and simmer for 20 minutes.
d) Add a spoonful of nut butter before serving.

Spicy South-western Breakfast Bowl

Makes: 1

NUTRITION: Calories 460|Fat 23g|Carbohydrates 24g|Sugars 1g |Protein 40g

INGREDIENTS:

- Extra virgin olive oil, for tossing
- Ghee, 1 teaspoon
- Pinch Salt and pepper
- fresh spinach, 3 cups
- chili powder, 1 teaspoon
- ½ red bell pepper, diced
- 1 avocado, pitted and diced
- 1 jalapeño, seeded and diced
- ½ green bell pepper, diced
- 2 sweet potatoes, peeled and diced
- 2 eggs
- ½ yellow onion, diced

INSTRUCTIONS:

a) Preheat the oven's temperature to 375 degrees Fahrenheit.
b) Arrange the sweet potatoes on a roasting sheet and drizzle with oil.
c) Season with salt, pepper, and chili powder.
d) Cook for 20 minutes while turning it once.
e) Cook the chicken bacon in another pant and set aside.
f) Add the onion, jalapeno, and peppers into the empty skillet and cook for 6 minutes.
g) Add the vegetables and cook them just until they wilt.
h) In a different skillet, melt the butter.
i) Crack in the eggs, and season with salt and pepper.
j) Place the sweet potatoes on the plate first, followed by the veggies, the egg, the crumbled bacon, and the avocado.

Coconut milk Oatmeal

Makes: 4

NUTRITION: Calories: 121| Fat: 3.2g | Carbohydrates: 17.8g | Sugars: 1.5g | Protein: 3.9g

INGREDIENTS:

- ground cinnamon, ½ teaspoon
- quick-cooking rolled oats, ½ cup
- ground ginger, ¼ teaspoon
- unsweetened coconut milk, ⅔ cup
- ground turmeric, ½ teaspoon

INSTRUCTIONS:

a) Combine milk and oats and microwave for about 1 minute.
b) Mix in the spices and microwave for another 2 minutes.
c) Serve with a garnish of your choice.

Asparagus and Soy milk Omelet

Makes: 4

NUTRITION: Calories 89| Fat 7g | Carbohydrate 2g| Protein 6g|Sugar: 1g

INGREDIENTS:

- 6 egg whites
- soy milk, 2 tablespoons
- sea salt, ¼ teaspoon
- black pepper, 1 pinch

- 6 asparagus spears, diced
- Butter, 2 tablespoons
- garlic powder, 1 pinch

INSTRUCTIONS:

a) Combine egg yolks, soy milk, and seasonings.
b) Cook the asparagus for about 5 minutes in the remaining butter.
c) Remove the asparagus from the skillet and place it to the side.
d) Add the leftover butter.
e) Cook the egg mixture for about 5 minutes.
f) Carefully raise the omelet with a spatula and turn it over.
g) Cook until the eggs are completely set, about 1 minute.
h) Spread asparagus over the egg before folding it.

Ginger pancakes

Makes: 4

NUTRITION: Calories: 60| Fat: 1g | Carbohydrates: 9.1g |Sugars: 1.7g | Protein: 3.5g

INGREDIENTS:

- chickpea flour, 1⅓ cups
- salt, to taste
- red chili powder, ½ teaspoon
- 1 green chili, seeded and chopped

- Water, 1 cup
- 1 piece of fresh ginger, grated
- Cooking spray
- cilantro leaves, chopped, 1 cup

INSTRUCTIONS:

a) In a sizable mixing dish, mash together the flour, salt, and chile pepper.
b) Stir in the ginger, cilantro, and pepper.
c) Include water and blend thoroughly.
d) Cover and leave standing for one and a half to two hours.
e) Spray cooking spray on a sizable nonstick pan, and add the required quantity of mix, tilting the skillet to spread it equally.
f) Cook each side for 10 to 15 seconds.
g) Repeat with the remaining mixture.

Avocado and Tomato Breakfast

Makes: 2

NUTRITION: Calories: 194 |Fat: 11 grams| Carbohydrates:20 grams |Protein: 5 grams|Sugar: 1g

INGREDIENTS:

- 1 avocado
- Flax Oil, 1 Tablespoon
- 1 clove of garlic, crushed
- Low-sodium salt, 1 pinch
- sesame seeds, 1 handful
- cherry tomatoes, diced, 1 handful
- ½ lemon

INSTRUCTIONS:

a) Combine all of the ingredients, then return to the avocado skin.
b) Sprinkle sesame seeds and salt on top before serving.

Omelet with mushrooms and peppers

Makes: 2

NUTRITION: Calories: 336|Fat: 27 g |Carbohydrates: 6 g| Sugar: 1 g | Protein: 17g

INGREDIENTS:

- 1 red bell pepper, sliced
- olive oil, extra-virgin, 2 tablespoons
- ⅛ teaspoon black pepper
- mushrooms, sliced, 1 cup
- 6 eggs, beaten
- ½ teaspoons sea salt

INSTRUCTIONS:

a) Heat the olive oil in a pan over medium-high heat.
b) Add red peppers and mushrooms, and cook the veggies for about 4 minutes, turning occasionally, until they are soft.
c) Mix the eggs, salt, and pepper in a medium combining dish.
d) Pour the eggs over the vegetables and let them cook for 3 minutes without moving, or until the edges of the eggs start to solidify.
e) Fold the egg in half using a spatula.

Tofu & Tomato Breakfast

Makes: 2

NUTRITION: Calories: 181| Carbohydrates: 9g | Protein: 10g | Fat: 11g | Sugar: 1g

INGREDIENTS:

- coconut oil, 1 tablespoon
- ½ onion, diced
- ½ cup regular firm tofu crumbled
- turmeric, 1 pinch
- 2 tomatoes, diced
- ½ red pepper
- Freshly ground black pepper, 1 pinch
- Sea salt, 1 pinch
- Basil leaves, 1 handful

INSTRUCTIONS:

a) Sauté onion in the coconut oil, then add the pepper.
b) Add tomatoes, tofu, and a pinch of turmeric.
c) Cook for 5 minutes, and then add the pepper, salt, and basil.

Walnut and almond porridge

Makes: 4

NUTRITION: Calories: 292 | Fat: 7.5g | Carbs: 9.6g | Sodium 75mg | Sugars: 1.2g | Protein: 8g

INGREDIENTS:

- chia seeds, ¼ cup
- Pecans, ½ cup
- sunflower seeds, ¼ cup
- Almonds, ½ cup
- Unsweetened coconut flakes, ¼ cup
- Unsweetened almond milk, 4 cups
- ginger powder, ¼ teaspoon
- powdered stevia, 1 teaspoon
- cinnamon powder, ½ teaspoon
- almond butter, 1 tablespoon

INSTRUCTIONS:

a) Combine pecans, almonds, and sunflower seeds in a food blender.
b) Boil the nut mixture for about 20 minutes while adding the chia seeds, coconut pieces, almond milk, spices, and stevia powder.
C) Add a spoonful of almond butter before serving.

Scrambled eggs with salmon

Makes: 4

NUTRITION: Calories: 236|Fat: 18 g |Carbohydrates: 1g| Sugar: 1g | Protein: 19g

INGREDIENTS:

• 8 eggs
• olive oil (extra-virgin), 2 tablespoons

• ¼ teaspoon black pepper
• 6 ounces of smoked salmon

INSTRUCTIONS:

a) In a skillet, heat the olive oil to a medium-high temperature.
b) Include the salmon, and simmer for 3 minutes, stirring occasionally.
c) In a mixing dish, combine the eggs and pepper.
d) Add them to the pan and gently toss them for about 5 minutes.

Seedy Breakfast

Makes: 2

NUTRITION: Calories 120|Total Fat 6g|Carbohydrates: 15g |Protein 4g|Sugar: 1g

INGREDIENTS:

• sesame seeds, 2 cups
• soy milk, 1½ tablespoons
• Almonds, 2 cups
• pumpkin seed, 2 cups

• sunflower seeds, 2 cups
• 1 grated apple
• water

INSTRUCTIONS:

a) Mix the seed mixture and grated apple and soak for three hours in water and soy milk.

Sugar-Free Granola

Makes: 4

NUTRITION: Calories: 180|Fat: 13g|Saturated Fat: 1g|Sodium: 40mg
|Carbohydrates: 15g|Sugars: 0g|Protein: 4g

INGREDIENTS:

- ground cinnamon, ½ teaspoon
- ¼ cup sugar-free maple syrup
- rolled oats, 3 cups
- vanilla extract, 1 teaspoon
- sunflower seeds, ¼ cup

- unsweetened shredded coconut, ¼ cup
- chopped nuts, ½ cup
- pumpkin seeds, ¼ cup
- sea salt, ¼ teaspoon
- coconut oil, melted, ¼ cup

INSTRUCTIONS:

a) Set the oven to 325ºF.
b) Combine Oats, almonds, seeds, and coconut.
c) Combine melted coconut oil, sugar-free maple syrup, vanilla essence, cinnamon, and
    sea salt in a different bowl.
d) Mix everything thoroughly.
e) Spread the ingredients out evenly on a baking pan.
f) Bake the granola until it turns golden brown and is crunchy for 25 to 30 minutes, tossing
    once or twice.
g) Before keeping it in an airtight receptacle, let the food cool entirely.
h) Top it with a sprinkling of fresh fruit or diced banana.

Cherry And Kale Smoothie

Makes: 2

NUTRITION: Calories: 187| Fat: 1.7g | Carbs: 44.2g | Protein: 4.2g|Sugars: 0g

INGREDIENTS:

- fresh cherries, pitted, 1 cup
- fresh kale, trimmed, 1 cup
- 1 teaspoon fresh ginger, peeled, and sliced or diced
- 2 ripe bananas, peeled and sliced
- 1 cup coconut water
- the ground cinnamon, ¼ teaspoon
- 1 tablespoon chia seeds, soaked for 15 minutes
- ground turmeric, ½ teaspoon

INSTRUCTIONS:

a) Place all components in a powerful blender and blend until well combined.
b) Immediately serve the smoothie in two cups.

Watercress Cranberry Smoothie

Makes: 2

NUTRITION: Calories 198|Fat 1g|Carbohydrates 47g|Protein 5g | Sodium18mg|Sugars 0g

INGREDIENTS:

- 2 cups watercress
- 1 cup of pineapple
- 1 ripe banana, sliced
- 1 orange, peeled and sliced or diced
- 1 pitted Medjool date (optional)
- 1 tablespoon powdered wheatgrass
- Purified water

INSTRUCTIONS:

a) Pour all the components into a blender, excluding the distilled water.
b) Add water for desired consistency.
c) Process until smooth.

Grape Berry Smoothie

Makes: 2

NUTRITION: Calories: 251|Fat: 4g|Carbohydrates: 53g|Protein: 19g |Sodium 11 mg|Sugars 0g

INGREDIENTS:

- seedless green grapes, ½ cup
- cinnamon powder, 1 teaspoon
- chia seeds, 2 tablespoons
- Baby spinach, 2 cups
- Raspberries, 1 cup
- 1 Medjool date (soften/soaked)
- ½ cup of water

INSTRUCTIONS:

a) Pour all the components into a blender, excluding the distilled water.
b) Add water to desired consistency. Process until smooth

Berry Cleanser Smoothie

Makes: 2

NUTRITION: Calories 202.4 |Fat 5 g | Saturated Fat 2 g |Sodium 36.5 mg | Carbohydrate 33 g| Protein 13 g|Sugars 0g

INGREDIENTS:

• 3 Swiss chard leaves, stems removed
• ¼ cup frozen cranberries
• Water, 1 cup

• ground flaxseed, 2 tablespoons
• 1 cup of raspberries
• 2 pitted Medjool date

INSTRUCTIONS:

a) Place all the components in a blender, and process until completely smooth.

Apple, beet, and strawberry smoothie

Makes: 2

NUTRITION: Calories: 400| Fat: 29.2g | Carbs: 36.7g | Protein: 1.7g |Sugars 0g

INGREDIENTS:

• 3 Medjool dates, pitted and chopped
• 1 cup frozen strawberries, peeled and sliced
• 1 beetroot, peeled and sliced or diced

• 1 cup apple, peeled, cored, and sliced
• ¼ cup extra-virgin coconut oil
• ½ cup almond milk, unsweetened

INSTRUCTIONS:

a) Combine everything and process until it's smooth.
b) Distribute the smoothie among the two cups.

Sugar-Free Berry Smoothie

Makes: 2

NUTRITION: Calories: 120|Fat: 1g|Sodium: 71mg| Carbohydrates: 27g
|Sugars: 0g|Protein: 3g

INGREDIENTS:

- vanilla protein powder, 1 scoop
- frozen mixed berries, 1 cup
- chia seeds, 1 teaspoon
- unsweetened almond milk, ½ cup
- Greek yogurt, ¼ cup

INSTRUCTIONS:

a) Blend everything until completely smooth.
b) Pour into a tumbler, then sip.
c) Expert Tip: To add more healthy fats and fiber to your smoothie, add a tablespoon of nut butter or a handful of spinach to the mix.

Cucumber-Mint Refresher

Makes: 2

NUTRITION: Calories: 20|Sodium: 11mg|Carbohydrates: 5g
|Sugars: 0g|Protein: 1g

INGREDIENTS:

- 1 cucumber
- Water, ½ cup
- 1 lime, peeled
- fresh mint leaves, ½ cup

INSTRUCTIONS:

a) Fill the blender jug with all the contents.
b) Blend for 10 seconds.
c) Serve over ice.

Apple Chile jam

NUTRITION: Calories: 11|Fat: 0g|Saturated Fat: 0g|Carbohydrates: 3g |Fiber: 0g|Sugars: 0g|Protein: 0g

INGREDIENTS:

- 1 red chili pepper, seeded and minced
- 2 apples, peeled, cored and chopped
- lemon juice, 2 tablespoons
- Salt, ¼ teaspoon
- Cinnamon, 1 teaspoon
- chia seeds, 2 tablespoons
- Water, ¼ cup

INSTRUCTIONS:

a) Combine the diced apples, minced chile pepper, water, lemon juice, cinnamon, and salt in a small saucepan.
b) Heat the combination to a boil over medium-high heat. When the apples are soft and the mixture has thickened, reduce the heat and simmer the mixture, stirring periodically, for an additional 15 to 20 minutes.
c) Turn off the heat and add the chia seeds to the skillet. Let the combination sit for five to ten minutes.
d) Transfer the liquid to a blender or food processor, and process until smooth.
e) Return the mixture to the pan and cook it for an additional 5 to 10 minutes over medium-high heat, stirring periodically, or until it reaches the desired jam-like consistency.
f) Take the jam off the fire and allow it to cool completely before putting it in a jar. Keep in the fridge for up to two weeks.

No-sugar Pear Sauce

NUTRITION: Calories: 40|Sodium: 0mg|Carbohydrates: 13g |Sugars: 1g|Protein: 0g

INGREDIENTS:

- Nutmeg, ¼ teaspoon
- Cinnamon, 1 teaspoon
- lemon juice, 1 teaspoon
- 4 large ripe pears, peeled and chopped
- Water, ½ cup

INSTRUCTIONS:

a) In a medium pot, mix the pear chunks with the water, lemon juice, cinnamon, and nutmeg.
b) Heat the combination to a boil over medium-high heat. Once the pears are soft and the mixture has thickened, reduce the heat and simmer the mixture, stirring periodically, for 15 to 20 minutes.
c) Remove the mixture from the heat and let it settle for five to ten minutes.
d) Transfer the liquid to a blender or food processor, and process until smooth.
e) Allow the pear sauce to completely cool before placing it in a jar. For up to two weeks, store in the refrigerator.

Blueberry Jam

NUTRITION: Calories: 10|Sodium: 0mg|Carbohydrates: 2.2g|Sugars: 1g |Protein: 0g

INGREDIENTS:

• lemon juice, 2 tablespoons
• chia seeds, 2 tablespoons

• fresh blueberries, 2 cups
• Water, ¼ cup

INSTRUCTIONS:

a) In a small pan over medium-high heat, heat the blueberries, water, and lemon juice for about 5 to 10 minutes, or until the blueberries have dissolved and the mixture is bubbling, stirring the mixture occasionally.
b) Take off the heat and stir in the chia seeds.
c) After letting the combination sit for five to ten minutes, transfer it to a blender or food processor and blend or process until smooth.
d) Store for up to two weeks in the refrigerator.

Cucumber-Mint Refresher

NUTRITION: Calories: 12|Fat: 0g|Sodium: 10mg|Carbohydrates: 2g |Sugars: 1g|Protein: 0g

INGREDIENTS:

• black pepper, ¼ teaspoon
• 2 large yellow onions, sliced thin
• olive oil,2 tablespoons

• Salt, ½ teaspoon
• Water, ¼ cup
• balsamic vinegar, ¼ cup

INSTRUCTIONS:

a) In a big skillet, warm the olive oil. Add onions.
b) Cook the onions, stirring periodically, for 15-20 minutes or until they are soft and caramelized.
c) Pour the water into the pan and stir in the balsamic vinegar, salt, and black pepper.
d) Decrease the heat to low, cover the pan, and simmer the combination for ten to fifteen minutes, stirring now and then, until the liquid has reduced and the mixture has thickened.
e) After turning off the heat, let the mixture cool in the pan for five to ten minutes.
f) Blend or process the items in a food processor to a smooth consistency.
g) Return the mixture to the skillet and cook for an additional 5 to 10 minutes, stirring periodically, until the jam-like consistency is achieved.

Low Sugar Hot Sauce

Makes: 4 (½-Pint) Jars

NUTRITION: Calories: 6|Sodium: 170mg|Carbohydrates: 1g
|Sugars: 1g|Protein: 0g

INGREDIENTS:

- Water, ¼ cup
- Honey, 1 tablespoon
- 15 hot peppers, stemmed and chopped
- 4 cloves garlic, minced
- Salt, ¼ teaspoon
- apple cider vinegar, ¼ cup

INSTRUCTIONS:

a) In a small saucepan, combine the coarsely chopped hot peppers, minced garlic, apple cider vinegar, water, honey, and salt.
b) Heat the combination to a boil over medium-high heat. Once the peppers are soft and the combination has thickened, reduce the heat and simmer the mixture, stirring periodically, for 10 to 15 minutes.
c) Remove the mixture from the heat and let it settle for five to ten minutes.
d) Transfer the liquid to a blender or food processor, and process until smooth.
e) Retain for up to two weeks in the refrigerator.

LEGUMES

Chickpea salad

Makes: 4

NUTRITION: Calories 302|Fat 17g|Carbohydrate 27g|Protein 10g |Sugars 1g

INGREDIENTS:

- 2 tablespoons olive oil
- 2 (19 ounces) canned chickpeas
- ½ green bell diced
- ¼ cup lemon juice

- parsley leaves, ¼ cup
- 1 Pinch salt
- 1 carrot, grated
- ½ red onion, diced
- black pepper, 1 pinch

INSTRUCTIONS:

a) Combine and thoroughly stir all of the components in a sizable mixing bowl.

Lentils and Zucchini

Makes: 2

NUTRITION: Calories: 125|Fat: 0.5|Carbohydrates: 25|Protein: 4.5 |Sugars: 1g

INGREDIENTS:

- ½ cup of dried lentils
- ½ lemon
- 2 garlic cloves
- 4 tomatoes, skinned
- 1 onion
- 1 pepper
- 1 piece of ginger
- 1½ cups Vegetable bouillon
- 1 zucchini
- A sprinkle of seeds
- Fresh basil
- Drizzle coconut oil

INSTRUCTIONS:

a) Simmer the lentils in the vegetable stock and the juice from ½ lemon.
b) Sauté onion using coconut oil.
c) Mix in the zucchini, garlic, peppers, tomatoes, and ginger, and simmer.
d) Add the legumes, herbs, and seeds last, adjusting the seasoning to taste.

Loaded Greens and Seeds

Makes: 3-4

NUTRITION: Calories: 140 Calories | Carbohydrates: 5g | Protein: 3g | Fat: 12g|Sugars: 1g

INGREDIENTS:

- Olive oil
- ½ green or red pepper
- cos lettuce, 1 bunch
- 1 handful of seeds & nuts
- ½ cucumber
- lamb's lettuce, 1 Handful
- 1 avocado
- salt & black pepper
- 2 bunches of baby spinach
- ½ can of chickpeas
- Tofu, 3½ ounces
- rocket leaves, 1 Handful
- 1 serving of quinoa, cooked
- Lemon
- 6 cherry tomatoes

INSTRUCTIONS:

a) Fry the tofu lightly in almond oil.
b) Toss everything together.

Broad Bean Salad with Turmeric Potatoes

Makes: 2

NUTRITION: Calories:254| Fat: 11.7g | Carbohydrates: 28.2g | Sugars: 1.3 g | Protein: 10.5g

INGREDIENTS:

- ½ cup broad beans
- ½ onion, sliced
- Diced cherry tomatoes, 1 handful
- parsley, basil, and chives, 1 handful each

- 4 tablespoons coconut oil
- sea salt, 1 pinch
- ½ cup new potatoes, sliced and parboiled
- Turmeric, 1 teaspoon

INSTRUCTIONS:

a) Heat half of the coconut oil and quickly sauté the onion and wide beans.
b) Season cherry tomatoes with salt and olive oil before setting them aside.
c) Fry the parboiled potatoes in extra coconut oil for five minutes. Spice with turmeric.
d) Combine the wide beans, tomato, potatoes, and olive oil in a dish.
e) Add salt and pepper for seasoning.

Low-Sugar Power Salad

Makes: 2

NUTRITION: Calories 330 |Fat 17.7g| Carbohydrates 1g|Sugar 0g | Protein 39.5g

INGREDIENTS:

- Romaine lettuce leaves
- Chickpeas, 1 can
- Asparagus, 1 bunch
- Olive oil
- 1 lemon, juiced

- 1 red pepper
- Baby spinach leaves
- 1 stick of celery
- 3 Roma tomatoes
- 1 avocado

INSTRUCTIONS:

a) Combine all of the ingredients.

Cucumber and Sprouts

Makes: 2

NUTRITION: 114 Calories|18.4g Carbohydrate|17g Protein| 1g Sugars

INGREDIENTS:

- spinach leaves, 2 Handfuls
- ½ Can chickpeas
- lettuce leaves, 1 Handful
- Sprouts, 2 handfuls
- 8 Cherry tomatoes
- ½ Cucumber

DRESSING:
- lime rind, 1 teaspoon
- Liquid Aminos, 1 teaspoon
- olive oil, 1 tablespoon
- 1-inch ginger, crushed
- orange rind, 1 tablespoon
- ½ lime juice

INSTRUCTIONS:

a) Steam the asparagus and snow peas on medium heat for 3 to 6 minutes.
b) Add salt, pepper, asparagus, and snow peas.
c) Drizzle lemon juice on the salad.

Aubergine, Potato & Chickpea

Makes: 2

NUTRITION: 196 Calories| Protein 8g| Carbohydrates 24g | Sugar 3g | Fat 8g

INGREDIENTS:

- ½ teaspoons cumin
- 1 can chickpeas
- 1 onion, peeled and finely sliced
- Coriander, 1 teaspoon
- 1 aubergine
- 1 potato
- 2 tablespoons coconut oil
- ¼ teaspoons turmeric
- Fresh coriander

SAUCE:
- 1 onion, peeled and finely sliced
- 2 teaspoons ginger, peeled and grated
- ½ teaspoons cumin
- 2 tablespoons coconut oil
- 6 whole cloves
- 450g plum tomatoes
- ¼ teaspoons turmeric
- Salt, 1½ teaspoons
- red chili powder, 1 teaspoon
- 3 cloves garlic, crushed

INSTRUCTIONS:

a) Cook cumin seeds and onion for three minutes.
b) Add the potato, aubergine, chickpeas, cumin, turmeric, and chopped coriander.
c) Add the garlic, ginger, and cloves, and cook for 60 seconds, then add the tomatoes, turmeric, and additional seasonings.
d) Using a hand mixer, blend the sauces until they are roughly combined.
e) Add veggies, coriander, water, salt, and pepper, and then serve.

BEANS, AND VEGETABLE SIDES

Almond Balsamic Beans

Makes: 4

NUTRITION: Calories: 315|Fat: 27g|Carbohydrates: 14.5g| Protein: 8g |Sugars: 1g

INGREDIENTS:

- ground almonds, 2 tablespoons
- olive oil, 1 tablespoon
- 1 pound green beans
- 1½ tablespoons balsamic vinegar

INSTRUCTIONS:

a) Steam the green beans with olive oil and balsamic vinegar.
b) Add the almonds, and serve.

Mango, Jalapeño & bean salad

Makes: 4

NUTRITION: Calories: 215| Fat: 7 g | Sodium: 128 Mg| Carbohydrate: 36 g |Protein: 7 g|Sugars: 1g

INGREDIENTS:

- 1 bell pepper, seeded, diced
- 15-ounce can of black beans, drained
- Low-Sodium Salt, 1 teaspoon
- black pepper, 1 teaspoon
- 2 green onions, sliced
- 15-ounce can, of low-sodium whole-kernel corn
- 1 cup avocado, cubed
- lime juice, 2 tablespoons
- 1 teaspoon chili powder
- 1 jalapeño pepper, diced
- olive oil, 1 tablespoon
- 2 mangos, cut into ½-inch cubes
- cilantro, chopped, 2 tablespoons
- Shredded lettuce

INSTRUCTIONS:

a) Distribute greens among the six plates.
b) Combine the corn, mango, avocado, onions, jalapenos, and black beans.
c) Combine and give the lime juice, olive oil, cilantro, chili powder, black pepper, and salt a good shake.
d) Pour dressing over lettuce and mixed greens and toss lightly to combine.
e) Add the mango-avocado combination on top.

Red Bean Stew from Jamaica

Makes: 4

NUTRITION: Calories 160| Fat 3g| Carbohydrate 30g| Protein 8g
|Sugar 0g

INGREDIENTS:

- Water, ½ cup
- black pepper, ¼ teaspoon
- 1 sweet potato, peeled and diced
- dried thyme, 1 teaspoon
- coconut milk, 13.5-ounce can
- cooked dark red kidney beans, 3 cups
- olive oil, 1 tablespoon
- ground allspice, ¼ teaspoon
- Low-Sodium Salt, ½ teaspoon
- diced tomatoes, 4.5-ounce can
- curry powder, 1 teaspoon
- 1 yellow onion, chopped
- 2 carrots, cut into slices
- 2 garlic cloves, minced

INSTRUCTIONS:

a) Heat the oil in a skillet before adding the onion and veggies and cooking for about 4 minutes.
b) Add the tomatoes, kidney beans, curry sauce, thyme, cardamom, garlic, sweet potato, and red pepper.
c) Stir in the water and simmer it in the covered pot for 30 minutes.
d) Just before serving, add the coconut milk.

Brussels Sprouts With Lemon

Makes: 6

NUTRITION: Calories 111|Fat 5g | Saturated 1g| Unsaturated 3g|Protein 7g
|Carbohydrates 15g|Fiber 6g|Sugars 1g |Added sugars 0g
|Sodium 232mg

INGREDIENTS:

- 2 pounds fresh Brussels sprouts, halved
- ¼ teaspoon black pepper
- 2 tablespoons shaved pecorino Romano
- kosher salt, ½ teaspoon
- lemon zest, 1 teaspoon
- lemon juice, 3 tablespoons
- Cooking spray
- ½ cup unsalted chicken stock
- ¼ cup pine nuts toasted

INSTRUCTIONS:

a) Combine the salt, broth, and Brussels sprouts in a slow cooker.
b) Cook for one hour and thirty minutes while covered on HIGH.
c) Coat a baking sheet with a rim or a broiler plate with cooking spray.
d) Using a slotted spatula, transfer the Brussels sprouts from the Crockpot to the hot broiler pan.
e) Sprinkle with pepper and drizzle with 2 teaspoons of lemon juice.
f) After 3 minutes of broiling, add the final 1 spoonful of lemon juice.
g) Garnish with cheese, lemon juice, and pine nuts.

FISH AND SEAFOOD

Salmon in Pesto

Makes: 4

NUTRITION: 270 Calories|20g Fat| 5g Carbohydrates|18g Protein|Sugar 0g

INGREDIENTS:

- 4 skinless salmon fillets
- olive oil, 2 teaspoons
- asparagus, ends trimmed, 1 bunch
- fresh lemon juice, 4 teaspoons, divided
- black pepper, ½ teaspoon, divided
- grape tomatoes, halved, 1 cup

PESTO
- raw hulled sunflower seeds, 1 teaspoon
- Salt, 1 teaspoon
- olive oil, 2 tablespoons
- black pepper, 1 teaspoon
- grated parmesan cheese, 1 tablespoon
- 1 clove garlic, chopped
- fresh basil leaves, ½ cup

INSTRUCTIONS:

a) Set the oven temperature to 400 degrees Fahrenheit.
b) In a food processor, combine basil, sunflower seeds, parmesan cheese, garlic, salt, and pepper.
c) While the food processor is running, drizzle two tablespoons of olive oil into the mixture until the sauce is smooth.
d) Toss the asparagus with pepper and 2 teaspoons of olive oil.
e) Place a fourth of the asparagus on a foil sheet. On top, one salmon fillet.
f) Spread 1 tablespoon of pesto on top of the fish and drizzle it with 1 teaspoon of lemon juice.
g) Sprinkle the halved tomatoes over the salmon.
h) Roll and crimp the edges of the foil around the sides of the package.
i) Repeat with the remaining ingredients to make four salmon packets in total.
j) Bake for 17 minutes on a baking sheet.

Citrus Poached Salmon

Makes: 3

NUTRITION: Calories: 259| Fat: 10.6g | Carbohydrates: 7.3g | Sugars: 1.4g | Protein: 33.4g

INGREDIENTS:

- coconut aminos, 3 tablespoons
- fresh ginger, finely grated, 1 teaspoon
- orange juice, ⅓ cup
- 3 garlic cloves, crushed
- 3 salmon fillets

INSTRUCTIONS:

a) Combine all the components in a bowl, excluding the salmon.
b) Cover the fish with the ginger and let it marinate for 15 minutes.
c) Cook the fish and ginger sauce in a pan over high heat.
d) Simmer for 12 minutes on medium heat.

Low-sugar Cod Ceviche

Makes: 4

NUTRITION: Calories: 119| Fat: 0.8g|Carbohydrate:7g|Protein: 21g |Sugar 0g

INGREDIENTS:

- Cod, cubed, 1 pound
- ground black pepper, ¼ teaspoon
- 2 red onions, separated into rings
- 1 clove fresh garlic, finely chopped
- Salt, ½ teaspoon
- 1 jalapeño pepper, split and cut into strips
- 1 head romaine lettuce, separated into leaves, washed
- lemon juice, 1 cup
- lime juice, 1 cup

INSTRUCTIONS:

a) Combine the onion, garlic, salt, and pepper with the lime and lemon juice before adding the marinade to the fish and letting it marinate for three hours.
b) Arrange a few washed and separated lettuce leaves on a platter to form the base of each dish.
c) Scoop the fish out of the marinade and place it on the cabbage leaves.

Paprika salmon

Makes: 4

NUTRITION: Calories: 175| Fat: 9.5g| Carbohydrates: 1 g| Sugars: 0.3 g | Protein: 22.2g

INGREDIENTS:

- ground coriander, ½ tablespoon
- Paprika, ½ teaspoon
- Pinch of salt
- ground cumin, ½ tablespoon
- ground ginger, ½ tablespoon
- coconut oil, melted, 1 tablespoon
- cayenne pepper, ¼ teaspoon
- fresh orange juice, 1 tablespoon
- 6 salmon fillets

INSTRUCTIONS:

a) Heat the gas barbecue and rub some oil on the grates.
b) Combine all the ingredients in a bowl, excluding the salmon, and mix until a paste develops.
c) Rub the paste over the salmon and marinate for 30 minutes in the refrigerator.
d) Grill fish for four minutes per side.

Lemon and Thyme Salmon

Makes: 4

NUTRITION: Calories 330 |Fat 18g| Carbohydrates 1g|Sugar 0g | Protein 39.5g

INGREDIENTS:

- 1 lemon, sliced thin
- Capers, 1 tablespoon
- Pinch low sodium salt and freshly ground pepper
- 32-ounce piece of salmon
- fresh thyme, 1 tablespoon
- Olive oil

INSTRUCTIONS:

a) Spread the fish on a parchment paper-lined baking sheet, skin side down.
b) Add salt and pepper for seasoning.
c) Place capers, lemon slices, and thyme on top of the fish.
d) Bake for 25 minutes at 400 degrees F.

Swiss Chard & Haddock

Makes: 1

NUTRITION: Calories: 402| Fat: 28.7g | Carbohydrates: 8.2g | Sugars: 1g | Protein: 29.5g

INGREDIENTS:

• 2 tablespoons almond oil
• fresh ginger, finely grated, 2 teaspoons
• 1 fillet of haddock
• coconut aminos, 1 teaspoon

• Salt and ground black pepper
• 2 garlic cloves, crushed
• Swiss chard, coarsely chopped, 2 cups

INSTRUCTIONS:

a) Melt 1 spoonful of almond oil in a saucepan.
b) Sauté the ginger and garlic for about a minute.
c) Add the haddock, salt, and pepper, and heat for 4 minutes on each side. Set aside
d) Sauté the chard, and coconut aminos in the leftover almond oil for about 8 minutes.
e) Serve salmon piece on a bed of chard.

Crusted Salmon with dill

Makes: 4

NUTRITION: Calories: 350| Fat: 28g | Carbohydrates: 5.2g | Sugars: 0.8 g | Protein: 24.9g

INGREDIENTS:

• 1 cup almonds, ground
• olive oil, 1 tablespoon
• black pepper, 1 pinch
• Dijon mustard, 4 tablespoons
• fresh dill, chopped, 1 tablespoon

• fresh lemon juice, 4 teaspoons
• fresh lemon zest, grated, 2 tablespoons
• garlic salt, ½ teaspoons
• 4 salmon fillets

INSTRUCTIONS:

a) Pulse the dill, lemon zest, garlic salt, black pepper, and butter into a crumbly mixture.
b) Layer salmon on a rimmed baking sheet
c) Spread Dijon mustard on top of each salmon fillet.
d) Spread the nut mixture evenly over each fillet.
e) Bake for about 15 minutes.

Low-Sugar Shrimp Scampi & Squash

Makes: 4

NUTRITION: Calories: 363 | Carbohydrates: 46g | Protein: 11g | Fat: 13g | Sugar: 2g

INGREDIENTS:

FOR THE SPAGHETTI:
- dried oregano, 1 teaspoon
- 1 spaghetti squash, softened and halved lengthwise
- Extra virgin olive oil, for drizzling
- Low sodium salt and pepper
- dried basil, 1 teaspoon

FOR THE SHRIMP SCAMPI:
- 8 ounces shrimp, peeled and deveined
- fresh parsley, 1 tablespoon
- 2 cloves garlic, minced
- extra virgin olive oil, 2 tablespoons
- Pinch of red pepper flakes
- Pinch salt and pepper
- Zest half a lemon
- Butter, 3 tablespoons
- Juice of 1 lemon

INSTRUCTIONS:

a) Set the oven's temperature to 400 F.
b) Set the squash halves on a baking tray with a rim.
c) Add a drizzle of oil and some spices.
d) Bake for 50 minutes in the microwave.
e) Use a fork to strand the zucchini by scraping the insides.
f) In a pan set over medium heat, melt the butter and olive oil.
g) Add the garlic and cook for three minutes.
h) Add the shrimp along with the salt, pepper, and pepper flakes and cook for 5 minutes.
i) Turn off the fire and stir in the spaghetti squash.
j) Add lemon juice and rind before tossing.
k) Add cilantro on top.

SOUPS AND STEWS

Tomato & Avocado Warmer

Makes: 2

NUTRITION: Calories 374| Fat 32g|Carbohydrates 21g|Protein 7g |Sugar 0g

INGREDIENTS:

- ¼ teaspoon dill seed
- 5 tomatoes
- 1 spring onion
- ¼ cup ground almonds
- 1 avocado
- Pinch cayenne
- 1 cup broth
- Sea salt & cracked black pepper

INSTRUCTIONS:

a) Blend all of the ingredients in a blender, aside from one tomato.
b) To serve, dice the remaining tomato and sprinkle it over top.

Raw Tomato & Basil Gazpacho

Makes: 2

NUTRITION: Calories 168 |Fat 12g |Carbohydrates 10g |Protein 2g |Sugar 0g

INGREDIENTS:

- 2 cups of freshly juiced tomatoes
- Olive oil
- 1 juiced cucumber
- ½ clove of garlic
- ¼ green pepper
- 1 stick of celery
- basil leaves, torn

INSTRUCTIONS:

a) In a mixing dish, combine the tomato and cucumber juices.
b) Add the celery, pepper, and garlic.
c) Add the basil stems and drizzle some extra virgin olive oil on top.
d) Season to flavor with salt and pepper.

Lentil & Butternut Squash Stew

Makes: 4

NUTRITION: 195 Calories| Protein 7.8g| Carbohydrates 24.2g | Sugar 2.1 g | Fat 8.3g

INGREDIENTS:

- wheat-free vegetable stock, 3 cups
- fresh dill, 2 tablespoons
- 2 white potatoes
- 1 stick of celery
- 4 carrots
- ½ butternut squash
- brown lentils, soaked, 1 cup
- tamari sauce, 1 teaspoon
- 2 brown onions
- 1 sweet potato
- fresh garden peas, 1 handful
- watercress, 1 handful

INSTRUCTIONS:

a) In a pan, bring stock and onions to a boil.
b) Add the carrot, potatoes, zucchini, and lentils. Simmer for 15 minutes.
c) Add the celery, green peas, dill, and fronds.

Coral lentil & Swiss chard soup

Makes: 4

NUTRITION: Calories 370|Fat 9g|Carbohydrates: 57g|Protein 20g|Sugar 0g

INGREDIENTS:

- 15-ounce can of diced tomatoes
- Swiss chard, coarsely chopped, 1 bunch
- cumin powder, 1 teaspoon
- turmeric powder, ½ teaspoon
- 2 carrots, diced
- sea salt, ½ teaspoons
- olive oil, 2 tablespoons
- 2 minced garlic cloves
- dried red lentils, 1 cup
- vegetable broth, 8½ cups
- 1 onion, diced
- red pepper flakes, ½ teaspoon
- ginger powder, ½ teaspoon

INSTRUCTIONS:

a) In a casserole pot, heat the oil.
b) Saute the onion and vegetables for seven minutes.
c) Add salt, chili pepper, garlic, ginger, cumin, and turmeric.
d) Add and cook the veggies for 5 minutes.
e) Add the broth and lentils and let it come to a boil.
f) Cook the legumes for 10 minutes with the lid on after reducing the heat to a simmer.
g) Add the chard and cook for an additional five minutes, or until it wilts.
h) Season with salt and pepper to taste.
i) Serve with a piece of lemon.

Roasted Lemon Herb Chicken

Makes: 4

NUTRITION: Calories: 405.3|Protein: 32.2g |Carbohydrates: 3.6g
|Sugars: 0.1g|Fat: 29.2g

INGREDIENTS:

- 12 total pieces of bone-in chicken thighs and legs
- 1 orange, sliced thin
- dried thyme, 1 teaspoon
- 1 onion, sliced thin
- dried rosemary, 1 tablespoon
- 1 lemon, sliced thin

FOR THE MARINADE:
- Italian seasoning, 1 tablespoon
- 2 cloves of garlic, minced
- low sodium salt and freshly ground pepper
- a few drops of stevia
- Juice of 1 lemon
- Juice of 1 orange
- red pepper flakes, 1 pinch
- extra virgin olive oil, 2 tablespoons
- onion powder, 1 teaspoon

INSTRUCTIONS:

a) Set the oven's temperature to 400 F.
b) In a dish, mix the marinade's components.
c) Add the poultry and marinate for three hours.
d) Transfer the poultry to a baking dish and surround it with slices of onion, orange, and lemon.
e) Season with low-sodium salt, pepper, thyme, and rosemary.
f) Bake for 30 minutes with a cover.
g) Remove the lid and simmer for an additional 30 minutes.

Creamy Baked Chicken

Makes: 4

NUTRITION: 193 Calories|7g Fat |12g Carbohydrates |2g Sugar |20g Protein

INGREDIENTS:

- Panko, ½ cup
- black pepper, 1 teaspoon
- 2 medium boneless, skinless chicken breasts, sliced lengthways
- Greek yogurt, ⅓ cup
- olive oil, 1 tablespoon
- onion powder, 1 teaspoon
- shredded low-fat cheddar cheese, ½ cup
- garlic powder, 1 teaspoon

INSTRUCTIONS:

a) Arrange your chicken on a well-oiled rimmed baking sheet.
b) Dredge with Greek yogurt.
c) Combine the dry ingredients in a small mixing bowl, then top the poultry with it.
d) Bake at 425 degrees for 12 minutes.

Lemon Garlic Chicken

Makes: 4

NUTRITION: Calories: 255|Protein: 30g|Fat: 12g|Carbohydrates: 2g |Fiber: 0g|Sugar: 0g

INGREDIENTS:

- Salt and pepper to taste
- fresh parsley, chopped, 1 tablespoon
- 4 boneless, skinless chicken breasts
- 2 cloves garlic, minced
- fresh lemon juice, ¼ cup
- olive oil, 2 tablespoons

INSTRUCTIONS:

a) Set your oven to 375°F.
b) Combine the lemon juice, olive oil, and garlic in a small dish.
c) Rub lemon-garlic mixture over chicken.
d) Season to flavor with salt and pepper.
e) Bake the chicken for 25 to 30 minutes.
f) Just before serving, garnish with fresh cilantro.

Chicken and Vegetable Stir-Fry

Makes: 4

NUTRITION: Calories: 259 |Protein: 28g|Carbohydrates: 10g|Fat: 12g |Fiber: 2g|Sugar: 6g|Sodium: 335mg

INGREDIENTS:

- olive oil, 2 tablespoons
- low-sodium soy sauce, 2 tablespoons
- 1 zucchini, sliced
- Salt and pepper to taste
- 1 yellow bell pepper, seeded and sliced
- 1 onion, sliced
- 1 pound boneless, skinless chicken breasts, cubed
- 2 cloves garlic, minced
- 1 red bell pepper, seeded and sliced

INSTRUCTIONS:

a) Heat the olive oil in a wok or big skillet over medium-high heat.
b) Add the chicken and heat for 5–7 minutes, or until it is browned all over.
c) Stir-fry the chicken with bell peppers, zucchini, onion, garlic, soy sauce, salt, and pepper for an additional 5-7 minutes, or until the veggies are tender.

Chicken with Avocado-Jalapeno Salsa

Makes: 4

NUTRITION: Calories: 345|Protein: 31g|Fat: 21g|Carbohydrates: 12g |Fiber: 8g|Sugar: 2g

INGREDIENTS:

- fresh cilantro, chopped, 2 tablespoons
- lime juice, 1 tablespoon
- Salt and pepper to taste
- 2 ripe avocados, diced
- olive oil, 1 tablespoon
- ½ red onion, diced
- ½ red bell pepper, diced
- 1 jalapeño pepper, seeded and minced
- 4 boneless, skinless chicken breasts

INSTRUCTIONS:

a) Set the heat on the griddle to medium-high.
b) Season poultry breasts with olive oil and salt and pepper.
c) Grill the poultry until it reaches a temperature of 165 degrees Fahrenheit, which will take 6 to 8 minutes on each side.
d) Combine chopped avocados, red onion, red bell pepper, jalapeno pepper, cilantro, and lime juice to make the avocado salsa.
e) Season with salt and pepper to taste.
f) Spoon salsa over the chicken before serving.

Beef and Mushroom Lettuce Wraps

Makes: 4

NUTRITION: Calories: 301|Fat: 22.2g|Saturated Fat: 7g|Sodium: 350mg
|Carbohydrates: 4g|Fiber: 1g|Sugars: 1g|Protein: 21g

INGREDIENTS:

- ground beef, 1 pound
- soy sauce, 1 tablespoon
- Salt and pepper to taste
- sesame oil, 1 tablespoon
- Lettuce leaves, for serving

- chili flakes, 1 teaspoon
- green onions, chopped, ¼ cup
- 2 cloves garlic, minced
- mushrooms, chopped, 1 cup

INSTRUCTIONS:

a) Brown the ground meat in a large skillet over medium heat.
b) Add the green onions, garlic, and mushrooms to the skillet and sauté until the onions are translucent and the mushrooms are tender.
c) To the skillet, add the soy sauce, sesame oil, chili flakes, salt, and pepper. Stir to incorporate.
d) Remove the meat mixture from the heat and serve it in lettuce leaves.

Beef and Vegetable Soup

Makes: 4

NUTRITION: Calories: 180|Fat: 7g|Saturated Fat: 3g|Sodium: 280mg |Carbohydrates: 10g|Sugars: 1.4g|Protein: 20g

INGREDIENTS:

- beef stew meat, 1 pound
- Salt and pepper to taste
- 1 onion, chopped
- dried thyme, 1 teaspoon
- low-sodium beef broth, 4 cups
- dried rosemary, 1 teaspoon
- celery, chopped, 2 stalks
- green beans, chopped, 1 cup
- 2 carrots, chopped

INSTRUCTIONS:

a) In a large pot over medium heat, brown the meat.
b) Place the celery, onion, and carrots in the pot and heat through.
c) Add the beef broth, green beans, thyme, rosemary, salt, and pepper.
d) Bring the stock to a boil before turning the heat down and letting it simmer for 30 to 40 minutes.

Coconut Ground Beef

Makes: 4

NUTRITION: Calories: 352| Fat: 22.8g | Carbs: 8.1g | Protein: 29.4g | Sugar: 0g

INGREDIENTS:

- 2 bay leaves
- 2 whole cloves
- 1 teaspoon of cumin
- 2 whole cardamoms
- Pinch of salt
- coconut oil, 2 tablespoons
- 1-pound lean ground beef
- ground cumin, 1 teaspoon
- garlic paste, ½ Tablespoons
- Water, ¼ cup
- fresh ginger paste, ½ Tablespoon
- 2 onions, chopped
- red chili powder, 1½ teaspoons
- coconut milk, 1 cup
- cinnamon stick, 1 piece
- ground turmeric, ⊠ teaspoon
- black pepper, freshly ground
- ground fennel seeds, 1½ teaspoons
- fresh cilantro, chopped, ¼ cup

INSTRUCTIONS:

a) Sauté the onion in the oil for 3 to 4 minutes while adding 2 tablespoons of salt.
b) Add the bay leaves, cumin, cardamom, cloves, and cinnamon stick to a skillet, and cook for 20 to 30 seconds.
c) Add the garlic and ginger puree, and simmer for an additional two minutes.
d) Add the beef, cooking it for about 4-5 minutes while breaking it up with a spatula.
e) Cook without the cover for about five minutes.
f) After adding the spices, stir constantly for 2 to 3 minutes.
g) Include the water and coconut milk, mix, and then simmer for 7-8 minutes.
h) Add salt and fresh cilantro before serving.

Beef Mushroom Yakisoba

Makes: 4

NUTRITION: Calories: 391|Fat: 16g|Sodium: 621mg|Carbohydrates: 41g |Sugars: 1g|Protein: 20.5g

INGREDIENTS:

- black pepper, to taste
- 1 cup broccoli slaw
- 3.5 ounces of shiitake mushrooms, sliced
- 1 lb. sirloin, flank steak, or skirt steak, cut into thin strips
- 14 ounces of millet and brown rice ramen noodles
- 1 clove garlic, minced
- ½ cup white onion, sliced
- 1 medium green pepper, sliced
- ½ cup snow peas, sliced in half lengthwise
- 5 teaspoons avocado oil, divided

BEEF YAKISOBA SAUCE:
- freshly grated ginger, 1 teaspoon
- rice vinegar, 1 tablespoon
- toasted sesame oil, 2 teaspoons
- 2 cloves garlic, finely chopped
- no added sugar ketchup, ¼ cup
- beef stock, 6 tablespoons
- low-sodium soy sauce, 3 tablespoons

GARNISH
- pickled ginger, sliced scallions, toasted sesame seeds, crushed red pepper flakes

INSTRUCTIONS:

FOR THE SAUCE
a) Combine the ginger, garlic, olive oil, ketchup, vinegar, soy sauce, and stock.

FOR THE NOODLES
b) Put a medium-sized saucepan of water on the stovetop to simmer.
c) Add the noodles to the saucepan once the water has boiled.
d) When the noodles are done boiling, rinse them completely.

FOR THE BEEF AND VEGGIES
e) Season the meat with black pepper.
f) Warm two teaspoons of oil in a pan over medium-high heat.
g) While stirring frequently, brown the meat for 4-5 minutes. Set away.
h) Heat the final 3 tablespoons of oil over medium-high heat.
i) Sauté the shiitake mushrooms and all the vegetables for 3 to 4 minutes.
j) Fill the pan with the cooked noodles, sauce, and pork.
k) Turn the stovetop heat up to high and stir frequently, letting everything absorb most of the sauce.
l) This should take no more than 2-3 minutes.
m) Garnish as desired and serve.

No-Sugar Ginger Beef and Broccoli

Makes: 3

NUTRITION: Calories: 321|Fat: 21g|Sodium: 601mg|Carbohydrates: 9g |Fiber: 2g|Sugars: 2g|Protein: 26g

INGREDIENTS:

BEEF AND BROCCOLI DISH
- lean sirloin, 1½ pounds
- arrowroot powder or corn starch, 1 tablespoon
- avocado oil, 3 tablespoons
- 3 green onions, diced
- minced garlic, 1 tablespoon
- 1 red bell pepper, seeded and diced
- chopped broccoli or broccolini, 2 cups
- sliced green onions and sesame seeds, for garnish

SAUCE
- low-sodium soy sauce, ¼ cup
- chicken broth, 1 cup
- minced fresh ginger, 1½ tablespoons
- arrowroot powder, 1 tablespoon

INSTRUCTIONS:

a) Dip the beef in cornstarch or arrowroot.
b) Heat a wok to a high temperature. Add the beef and oil once it's hot.
c) Cook for about 5 minutes or until you see sear marks.
d) After that, take it out of the pan and set it aside.
e) Reduce the heat of the pan to medium and add the oil, garlic, and green onion. Cook for about 2 minutes or until aromatic.
f) Cook for an extra 2 minutes after adding pepper.
g) Add chopped broccoli or broccolini and cover the pan for two to three minutes.
h) Combine the ingredients for the sauce, pour it in, and immediately combine.
i) Garnish with sesame seeds and green onion.
j) Enjoy with jasmine rice or cauliflower rice.

PORK

Pork Loin With Port And Rosemary Sauce

Makes: 4-6

NUTRITION: Calories 296|Fat 11g | Saturated 5g| Unsaturated 4g
|Protein 28g|Carbohydrates 18.2g|Fiber 3g|Sugars 2g
|Sodium 664mg

INGREDIENTS:

- boneless pork loin, 3 pounds
- kosher salt, ¼ teaspoon
- 24-ounce package of frozen steam-and-mash potatoes
- 28-ounce can of no-salt-added crushed tomatoes, undrained
- half-and-half, 6 tablespoons

- 8 garlic cloves, halved lengthwise
- 2 fresh rosemary sprigs
- unsalted butter, 4 tablespoons
- Port, ½ cup
- crème fraîche, 6 tablespoons
- olive oil, 1 tablespoon
- anchovy paste, 2 teaspoons
- black pepper, 1 teaspoon

INSTRUCTIONS:

a) Cut 16 little pockets around the pork midsection, and stuff the garlic into the pockets.
b) Sprinkle salt and pepper all over the pork loin.
c) In a nonstick skillet, heat the oil over medium heat until it shimmers, about one minute.
d) Brown the pork loin on all sides.
e) Transfer the pork to a Stewing pot, saving the drippings in the skillet.
f) Add the anchovy paste and rosemary, and cook for around 1 minute.
g) To remove the browned bits from the skillet's bottom, add the port.
h) Add the tomatoes and ½ teaspoon of salt to the mixture that has been transferred to the slow cooker.
i) For about three hours, slow cook the pork until a thermometer inserted into the thickest part registers 140°F.
j) Reserving the Crockpot's cooking liquid, transfer the pork to a cutting board or serving platter; The pork should rest for ten minutes.
k) In a saucepan, pour the reserved cooking liquid.
l) Bring to a simmer over low heat; boil for roughly eight minutes.
m) Prepare the potatoes as directed on the package, omitting the butter and milk.
n) To the steamed potatoes, add the crème fraîche, half-and-half, 2 tablespoons of butter, the remaining ¼ teaspoon salt, and ½ teaspoon pepper; mash to the ideal consistency.
o) Stir the excess 2 tablespoons of the margarine into the diminished sauce until liquefied.
p) Serve the sliced pork with the reduced sauce and potatoes.

Slow Cooker Pulled Pork

Makes: 4

NUTRITION: Calories 182 |Carbohydrates 0.1g |Sugar 0.1 g |Protein 24 g |Fat 8g |Sodium 75 mg

INGREDIENTS:

- coconut aminos, 1 tablespoon
- ground cumin, 1 teaspoon
- onion powder, 1 tablespoon
- apple cider vinegar, ¼ cup
- Pepper, 1 teaspoon
- garlic powder, 1 tablespoon
- tomato paste, 1 tablespoon
- Salt, 1 teaspoon
- shoulder pork roast, 1 pound
- Paprika, 1 teaspoon

INSTRUCTIONS:

a) Combine the seasonings, coconut aminos, and tomato paste in a small dish.
b) Skin side down put the pork roast in the slow cooker. Cover the roast thoroughly with the seasoned paste.
c) Turn the roast over so the skin side is now facing up. Pour the vinegar into the slow cooker from the side, not directly on top of the roast.
d) Cover the slow cooker and cook for 10 to 12 hours.
e) After the roast has finished cooking, shred it and return the flesh to the juice to rest for 10 to 15 minutes.

Bacon, Leek, Thyme Farro

Makes: 4-6

NUTRITION: Calories 158|Fat 2g | Saturated 1g| Unsaturated 1g |Protein 9g|Carbohydrates 26g|Fiber 3g |Sugars 1g |Sodium 331mg

INGREDIENTS:

- 4 bacon slices, chopped
- sliced thin fresh cremini mushrooms, 2 cups
- kosher salt, ¾ teaspoon
- black pepper, ½ teaspoon
- unsalted chicken stock, 3 cups
- uncooked farro, 1½ cups
- minced garlic, 1 tablespoon
- Gruyère cheese, grated, 1 ounce
- sliced thin leeks, 1½ cups
- chopped fresh thyme, 1 tablespoon

INSTRUCTIONS:

a) Cook the pork for about 5 minutes on medium heat in a nonstick pan.
b) Transfer the bacon to a platter lined with paper towels, retaining the bacon drippings in the skillet.
c) To the hot drippings in the skillet, add the leeks and mushrooms. Cook, stirring frequently, for 6 to 8 minutes, or until they are soft and slightly browned.
d) Add the thyme and garlic, and cook them for one minute, stirring regularly, until fragrant.
e) A Crockpot should be filled with the onion mixture.
f) Add the stock, farro, salt, and pepper, and cook on high for about two hours, covered. After ten minutes, turn off the Crockpot and let the combination cool.
g) Serve with bacon and cheddar cheese on top.

Ground Pork Stir Fry

Makes: 4

NUTRITION: Calories: 415| Carbohydrates: 4g | Protein: 20g | Fat: 34g | Fiber: 1g | Sugar: 1g

INGREDIENTS:

- Sesame Oil, 2 tablespoons
- ground pork, 1 pound
- Soy Sauce, 1 tablespoon
- olive oil, 1 tablespoon
- Minced Ginger, 1 tablespoon
- 2 Green Chili sliced
- Chopped Green Scallions, ½ cup
- 1 head of butter lettuce
- chopped cilantro, ½ cup
- Sambal Olek, 2 teaspoons
- Minced Garlic, 1 tablespoon
- Lemon Juice, 1 tablespoon

INSTRUCTIONS:

a) Add oil to a 10-inch pan over medium-high heat. To the hot oil, add minced ginger and garlic and let them sizzle for 2-3 seconds. Include the pork rinds.

b) Brown the meat, separating every one of the clusters.

c) When the meat is almost done after about 8 minutes, push it to the sides to make a small space in the middle. Sliced red and green chilis should be added.

d) Stir in the sesame oil, soy sauce, and, if desired, the sambal olek.

e) Remove the pork from the heat and allow it to rest for three to four minutes uncovered to slightly cool.

f) Add the cilantro and chopped green onions. Stir in the lemon juice thoroughly.

g) Divide the butter lettuce leaves among plates and add the spicy pork mixture.

White Bean–And–Sausage Cassoulet

Makes: 4

NUTRITION: Calories 404|Fat 18g | Saturated 5g| Protein 19g |Carbohydrates 42g|Fiber 11g|Sugars 3g |Sodium 570mg

INGREDIENTS:

- Crumbled Italian pork sausage, 6 ounces
- chopped yellow onion, ¾ cup
- unsalted chicken stock, 1 cup
- black pepper, ¾ teaspoon
- kosher salt, ⅛ teaspoon
- olive oil, 2 teaspoons
- 2 tablespoons, plus 1 teaspoon of chopped fresh thyme
- 14½-ounce can of no-salt-added fire-roasted diced tomatoes, undrained
- tomato paste, 2 tablespoons
- 30 ounces of cannellini beans, drained, rinsed, and mashed slightly
- chopped celery, ¼ cup
- matchstick carrots, ¼ cup
- panko toasted, ⅓ cup

INSTRUCTIONS:

a) In a nonstick pan over medium heat, sauté the sausage for about 2 minutes.
b) Cook for an additional 5 minutes after adding the onion, carrots, celery, and 2 teaspoons of thyme.
c) Add tomato paste, tomatoes, pepper, salt, and other seasonings; heat to a simmer.
d) Add the chicken broth and move the sausage mixture to a 6-quart Crockpot.
e) To the Crockpot, add the mashed beans.
f) Cook on medium for four hours.
g) Serve the sausage mixture, then top with toasted panko and fresh thyme.

Spicy Plum-Glazed Meatballs

Makes: 4

NUTRITION: Calories 415|Fat 12g | Saturated 4g| Unsaturated 7g |Protein 28g|Carbohydrates 47g|Fiber 2g|Sugars 2g |Sodium 677mg

INGREDIENTS:

- 1 pound lean ground pork
- minced fresh ginger, 2 teaspoons
- 2 cups jasmine rice, cooked
- 1 egg, lightly beaten
- black pepper, ¼ teaspoon
- Cooking spray
- 2 tablespoons rice vinegar

- ⅓ cup of no-sugar plum sauce
- ¼ cup water
- ½ cup panko
- 3 tablespoons scallions, finely chopped
- low-sodium soy sauce, 2½ tablespoons
- 1 tablespoon Sriracha chili sauce

INSTRUCTIONS:

a) In a bowl, gently mix the pork, panko, egg, scallions, and pepper until well combined.
b) Create 24 meatballs out of the mixture.
c) The meatballs should be placed in a Crockpot that has been sprayed with cooking oil.
d) In a dish, combine the plum sauce, water, soy sauce, ginger, Sriracha, and the other ingredients. Then, pour the mixture over the meatballs.
e) Cook the meatballs covered on HIGH for approximately 1 hour and 30 minutes.
f) While leaving the sauce mixture in the Crockpot, use a slotted spoon to move the meatballs to a tray.
g) Strain the sauce combination into a skillet, discarding the sediments as you go.
h) Bring the sauce mixture to a boil while stirring periodically over high heat.
i) Cook the glaze for about 4 minutes, stirring occasionally, or until it has diminished.
j) Add the rice vinegar and whisk, then add the meatballs.
k) Serve and enjoy.

Pork Posole

Makes: 4-8

NUTRITION: Calories 311|Fat 12g | Saturated 4g| Unsaturated 7g |Protein 31g|Carbohydrates 17g|Fiber 4g|Sugars 1g |Sodium 645mg

INGREDIENTS:

- 3-pound lean boneless pork shoulder, trimmed and cut into 1½-inch pieces
- 15-ounce can of no-salt-added pinto beans, drained and rinsed
- 15-ounce can of white hominy, drained and rinsed
- kosher salt, 1 teaspoon
- unsalted chicken stock, 4 cups
- chopped yellow onions, 1½ cups
- sliced thin scallions
- Fresh oregano leaves
- sliced thin radishes
- salsa Verde, 1 cup
- black pepper, 1 teaspoon
- canola oil, 1 tablespoon
- ground cumin, 1 tablespoon
- chopped poblano chiles, 1½ cups

INSTRUCTIONS:

a) Rub the cumin, salt, and black pepper over the pork. In a pan over medium heat, warm the oil. Cook the pork in the skillet for about 4 minutes, stirring periodically, until it turns golden brown.
b) Move into a Crockpot and cook for 5 minutes.
c) After about 5 minutes, add the onions and poblano chiles and gently caramelize.
d) Add ½ cup of the stock and stir to loosen the browned pieces.
e) Add the leftover stock, hominy, pinto beans, and salsa Verde.
f) Slow-cook the pork for about 7½ hours, or until it is soft.
g) Use a potato masher to mash some of the legumes and hominy.
h) Add sliced radishes, scallions, and oregano leaves to the broth before serving.

Lamb with peas

Makes: 4

NUTRITION: Calories: 226| Fat: 9.7g | Carbs: 6.4g | Protein: 27.2g|Sugar 0.1 g

INGREDIENTS:

- 3 dried red chilies
- 1 cinnamon stick
- 2 bay leaves
- 1-pound lean ground lamb
- ½ cup Roma tomatoes, chopped
- 4 garlic cloves, crushed
- ground coriander, 1½ teaspoons
- fresh cilantro, chopped, ¼ cup
- ground turmeric, ½ teaspoon
- ground cumin, ½ teaspoon
- 1 red onion, diced
- ground nutmeg, ¼ teaspoon
- 1½ cups of water
- 3 green cardamom pods
- ½ teaspoon cumin
- ½ cup shelled fresh peas
- Salt and ground black pepper
- 1-piece ginger, chopped
- Whipped plain yogurt, 2 tablespoons
- 1 tablespoon coconut oil
- ½ teaspoon garam masala powder

INSTRUCTIONS:

a) In a Dutch oven, heat the oil and cook the onion for three to four minutes, stirring occasionally.
b) Add and cook the ginger, garlic, spice blend, and bay leaf for one minute.
c) Add the meat and cook it for five more minutes.
d) Add the tomatoes and cook for 10 minutes, stirring periodically.
e) Add water and green peas; simmer for 25 to 30 minutes on medium heat.
f) Cook for 4 to 5 minutes, adding yogurt, cilantro, salt, and black pepper.

Lamb Chops with Herb Rub

Makes: 4

NUTRITION: Calories: 358 |Protein: 33g|Carbohydrates: 1g|Fat: 25g |Fiber: 0g|Sugar: 0g|Sodium: 142mg

INGREDIENTS:

- dried thyme, 1 teaspoon
- 4 lamb chops (4-6 ounces each)
- dried oregano, 1 teaspoon
- 1 tablespoon olive oil
- Salt and pepper to taste
- garlic powder, 1 teaspoon

INSTRUCTIONS:

a) Turn the grill's heat up to medium-high.
b) Brush lamb steaks with olive oil and season with salt, pepper, oregano, thyme, and garlic powder.
C) Grill for 4-6 minutes on each side, or until it's cooked to your preference.

Basil Turkey with Roasted Tomatoes

Makes: 2

NUTRITION: Calories 328|Fat 14.2 g| Carbohydrate 23 g| Sugars 3 g | Protein 26 g

INGREDIENTS:

- 2 turkey breasts
- a few drops of stevia
- Fresh parsley, for garnish
- extra virgin olive oil, 2 tablespoons
- sliced thin fresh basil, ½ cup
- mushrooms, chopped, 1 cup
- ½ medium onion, chopped
- low sodium salt and pepper
- 1-pint cherry tomatoes

INSTRUCTIONS:

a) Set the oven's temperature to 400 F.
b) Arrange the tomatoes on a baking tray and dress them with a mixture of stevia, olive oil, salt, and pepper.
c) Bake until tender for 17 minutes.
d) In a saucepan over medium heat, melt one tablespoon of olive oil. Add and cook the mushrooms and onions for 12 minutes.
e) Salt and pepper the poultry before putting it in the pan.
f) Simmer for 15 minutes.
g) Divide the tomatoes between two serving dishes.
h) Place a turkey breast on each dish, then garnish with parsley, onions, mushrooms, and pan drippings.

Turkey and Vegetable Stir Fry

Makes: 4

NUTRITION: Calories: 284|Protein: 41g|Carbohydrates: 14g|Fat: 8g |Fiber: 5g|Sugar: 11g|Sodium: 418mg

INGREDIENTS:

- low-sodium soy sauce, ¼ cup
- sliced mixed vegetables, 2 cups
- Honey, 1 tablespoon
- Salt and pepper to taste
- grated ginger, 1 tablespoon
- ground turkey, 1 pound
- 2 cloves garlic, minced
- olive oil, 1 tablespoon

INSTRUCTIONS:

a) In a big skillet, heat the olive oil over a medium-high fire.
b) Add the ground turkey and cook it, breaking it up into small bits, until it is browned.
c) Stir-fry the mixed veggies for 3–4 minutes, or until they are crisp-tender, in the skillet with the garlic and ginger.
d) Combine soy sauce and honey in a different dish.
e) Add the sauce to the skillet and stir-fry for an extra 2 to 3 minutes.
f) Season with salt and pepper.

Spicy Lamb and Veggie Skewers

Makes: 4

NUTRITION: Calories: 296 |Protein: 27g|Carbohydrates: 10g|Fat: 17g |Fiber: 3g|Sugar: 1g|Sodium: 75mg

INGREDIENTS:

- Paprika, 1 tablespoon
- ½ teaspoon cayenne pepper
- olive oil, 1 tablespoon
- Salt and pepper to taste
- 1 pound boneless lamb, cut into 1-inch cubes
- mixed vegetables, 2 cups

INSTRUCTIONS:

a) Turn the grill's heat up to medium-high.
b) Mix the olive oil, paprika, cayenne, salt, and pepper, and add the lamb pieces. Let it marinate.
c) Thread lamb and mixed vegetables onto skewers, alternating between the two.
d) Grill skewers for 6-8 minutes, turning occasionally, until lamb is cooked to your desired doneness.

Lamb and Lentil Stew

Makes: 4

NUTRITION: Calories: 326 |Protein: 28g|Carbohydrates: 28g |Fat: 11g|Fiber: 12g|Sugar: 1g|Sodium: 417mg

INGREDIENTS:

- dried rosemary, 1 teaspoon
- olive oil, 2 tablespoons
- low-sodium chicken broth, 2 cups
- 2 cloves garlic, minced
- 1 onion, chopped
- dried lentils, 1 cup
- Salt and pepper to taste
- 1 pound boneless lamb, cut into 1-inch cubes
- low-sodium diced tomatoes, 1 can

INSTRUCTIONS:

a) Heat the olive oil to a medium-high temperature.
b) Add the lamb pieces and brown them thoroughly.
c) Add the onion and garlic to the saucepan and cook for 3–4 minutes, or until soft.
d) Fill the pot with lentils, diced tomatoes, chicken stock, rosemary, salt, and pepper.
e) Cook for one to two hours on low heat after bringing it to a boil.

Maple-Mustard Glazed Turkey Breast

Makes: 4-6

NUTRITION: Calories 251|Fat 3g | Saturated 1g| Unsaturated 2g |Protein 43g|Carbohydrates 10g|Fiber 0g|Sugars 1.2g |Sodium 367mg

INGREDIENTS:

- Dijon mustard, 2 tablespoons
- black pepper, ¼ teaspoon
- low-sugar apple cider, 1 cup
- 3 fresh thyme sprigs
- 6-pound whole bone-in turkey breast
- kosher salt, 1 teaspoon
- low-sugar apple cider vinegar, 1 tablespoon
- pure maple syrup, ⅓ cup
- Water, 2 tablespoons
- Fresh thyme leaves
- unsalted chicken stock, ½ cup
- Cornstarch, 5 teaspoons

INSTRUCTIONS:

a) Bring apple cider and thyme stems to a boil. Discard the thyme sprigs.
b) Add the mustard and maple syrup.
c) Put the poultry in a Crockpot that holds 6 quarts.
d) Rub ¼ teaspoon of salt under the skin,
e) Spread the apple cider mixture over the poultry.
f) Cook on HIGH for about 3 hours and 30 minutes with the cover on.
g) Add thyme stems as a garnish.

Low-Sugar Tuna Salad

Makes: 4

NUTRITION: 312 Calories| Protein 38.8g|Carbohydrates 6.5g |Sugars 1.4g| Fat 13.6g

INGREDIENTS:

- 10 sun-dried tomatoes, softened and diced
- extra virgin olive oil, 2 Tablespoons
- lemon juice, ½ Tablespoon
- 1 clove of garlic, minced
- finely chopped parsley, 3 Tablespoons
- 2 (5 oz) cans of tuna, flaked
- 2 ribs of celery, diced finely
- Pinch low sodium salt and pepper

INSTRUCTIONS:

a) Combine the diced celery, tomatoes, extra virgin olive oil, garlic, parsley, and lemon juice with the tuna.
b) Season with pepper and low-sodium salt.

Tomato and basil salad

Makes: 4

NUTRITION: Calories: 141|Fat: 14.2 g | Carbohydrates: 4g | Sugar: 3g | Protein: 1g

INGREDIENTS:

- 4 heirloom tomatoes, chopped
- basil leaves, ¼ cup
- 2 garlic cloves, crushed
- ¼ cup olive oil (extra-virgin)

- ½ teaspoons sea salt
- ¼ teaspoon black pepper, freshly ground

INSTRUCTIONS:

a) Combine everything in a bowl.

Carrot, Spinach & Almond Salad

Makes: 2

NUTRITION: 94 Calories|16.4g Carbohydrate|15.5g Protein|Sugar 0.1 g

INGREDIENTS:

- 1 bunch of baby spinach leaves
- 2 spring onions, cut lengthways
- 1 carrot
- ¼ grapefruit
- 1 clove of garlic, minced

- Juice of ½ lemon
- ¼ red cabbage shredded
- Sliced almonds, 1 handful
- Olive oil

INSTRUCTIONS:

a) In a salad bowl, combine all of the vegetables.
b) Garnish with lemon juice and oil.

Cabbage and Carrot Coleslaw

Makes: 2

NUTRITION: 94 Calories|16.4g Carbohydrate |15.5g Protein|Sugar 1 g

INGREDIENTS:

• ½ red cabbage shredded
• ½ green cabbage shredded
• 1 carrot, sliced thin
• 1 courgette, sliced thin

• Handful of parsley
• ½ lime
• 1 chili
• 2 tablespoons of avocado oil
• Himalayan salt

INSTRUCTIONS:

a) Combine everything in a mixing bowl.
b) Enjoy.

Olive and Kale Salad

Makes: 2

NUTRITION: Calories:214| Fat: 17g | Carbohydrates: 23g | Sugars: 1.3 g | Protein: 10.5g

INGREDIENTS:

• 2 carrots, grated
• 3 handfuls of cherry tomatoes, halved
• A few dashes of Aminos
• Sun-dried tomatoes Goat's cheese
• 1 red onion, sliced
• ½ cup soaked pine nuts
• 1 bunch of Kale, shredded

• sesame seeds, ¼ cup
• Raw black olives halved
• olive oil, ¼ cup
• 1 lemon, juiced
• A pinch of salt
• A pinch of black pepper

INSTRUCTIONS:

a) Combine all of the ingredients in a mixing dish.

Low-Sugar Asparagus Salad

Makes: 2

NUTRITION: 83 calories| protein 4.5g| carbohydrates 4g | Sugars 1.7g | fat 5.7g

INGREDIENTS:

• Grated lemon peel
• Fresh thyme
• Fresh lemon juice of 1 lemon

• 12 asparagus stems, steamed
• 8 spring onions, steamed
• melted Avocado butter, 2 tablespoons

INSTRUCTIONS:

a) Combine the lemon zest, juice, and thyme with the avocado butter.
b) Dress the asparagus and spring onion.

Spinach and Walnut Salad

Makes: 4

NUTRITION: Calories: 491|Fat: 50.4 g |Carbohydrates: 9 g| Sugar: 1 g | Protein: 11g

INGREDIENTS:

• 4 cups fresh baby spinach
• ¼ cup chopped walnuts

• ¼ cup raspberry vinaigrette

INSTRUCTIONS:

a) Combine spinach and walnuts in a medium dish.
b) Dress with a vinaigrette and serve right away.

Turkey Bacon and Broccoli Salad

Makes: 4

NUTRITION: Calories 407| Fat 39g| Carbohydrate 12g| Protein 8g |Sugar 1 g

INGREDIENTS:

- 3 slices of turkey bacon
- sliced almonds, ½ cup
- halved cherry tomatoes, ½ cup
- cauliflower florets, ½ cup
- ½ green bell pepper, sliced in rings
- broccoli florets, 2 cups
- Almond mayonnaise

INSTRUCTIONS:

a) Cook turkey bacon according to package instructions, then drain on paper towels.
b) In a large mixing bowl, combine the broccoli, cauliflower, tomatoes, and almonds; stir with ½ cup of the Almond mayonnaise.
c) Garnish with bacon and green pepper rings and serve cold.

Cheesy Lemon Quinoa Salad

Makes: 4

NUTRITION: 250 Calories|8g Fat |3g Saturated|262mg Sodium | 32g Carbohydrates|1g Sugar|9g Protein

INGREDIENTS:

- Pinch teaspoon salt
- Juice of ½ lemon
- 2 cloves garlic, pressed
- 1 tablespoon dill, chopped
- olive oil, 2 tablespoons
- 1 small yellow bell pepper, diced
- quinoa, cooked, 1 cup
- black pepper, 1 teaspoon
- cherry tomatoes, quartered, 1 cup
- 1 cucumber diced
- reduced-fat feta cheese, crumbled, 1 cup

INSTRUCTIONS:

a) Mix olive oil, garlic, lemon juice, salt, and pepper.
b) Toss everything with the dressing.

Stir-Fried Vegetables & Rice

Makes: 4

NUTRITION: Calories 161| Fat 3g | Carbohydrate 31g| Protein 8g|Sugar 1 g

INGREDIENTS:

- 1 onion, chopped
- Turmeric, ½ teaspoon
- 2 green onions, minced
- 1 zucchini, chopped
- 2 garlic cloves, minced
- Peas, 1 cup
- toasted sesame oil, 1 tablespoon
- grape-seed oil, 2 tablespoons
- long-grain rice, cooked, 3 cups
- 1 carrot, chopped
- grated fresh ginger, 2 teaspoons
- soy sauce, 2 tablespoons
- dry white wine,2 teaspoons

INSTRUCTIONS:

a) In a pan over medium heat, add the oil and cook the onion, carrot, and zucchini for about 5 minutes.
b) Stir in the green scallions, garlic, and ginger for about 3 minutes.
c) Stir for about 5 minutes while adding the rice, peas, soy sauce, and wine.
d) Add a sesame oil drizzle.

Broccoli Cauliflower Fry

Makes: 2

NUTRITION: 196 Calories| Protein 8g| Carbohydrates 24g | Sugar 2.1 g | Fat 8.3g

INGREDIENTS:

- assorted sprouts, 1 handful
- 3 spring onions
- 1 garlic clove, chopped Liquid Aminos
- Wild/brown rice
- 4 broccoli florets
- 1 pepper
- 4 cauliflower florets

INSTRUCTIONS:

a) Cook the rice in a vegetable stock that is yeast-free.
b) Steam the onion and garlic for three minutes.
c) Toss in the remaining ingredients and simmer for a few minutes more.

Low-Sugar Ratatouille

NUTRITION: 197 Calories| Protein 8g| Carbohydrates 24g | Sugar 1g | Fat 8g

INGREDIENTS:

- olive oil, 2 tablespoons
- 1 yellow bell pepper, diced
- 1 onion, diced
- Salt and pepper to taste
- dried oregano, 1 teaspoon
- 3 garlic cloves, minced
- 1 zucchini, diced
- 1 eggplant, diced
- 1 red bell pepper, diced
- 1 yellow squash, diced
- 14-ounce can of diced tomatoes
- dried thyme, 1 teaspoon

INSTRUCTIONS:

a) In a large skillet or Dutch oven, warm the olive oil over medium heat.
b) Cook the onion and garlic until soft, about 5 minutes.
c) Fill the skillet with the eggplant, zucchini, yellow squash, and red and yellow bell peppers.
d) Cook the vegetables for 10 to 12 minutes, or until they are fork-tender.
e) Add the salt, pepper, dried thyme, dried oregano, and diced tomato can to the skillet.
f) Simmer for 5 to 10 minutes, or until well combined.

Tomato & Cauliflower Spaghetti

Makes: 4

NUTRITION: 157 Calories| Protein 7.8g| Carbohydrates 24.2g | Sugar 1 g | Fat 8.3g

INGREDIENTS:

- 1 tablespoon olive oil
- 125g sun-blushed tomatoes, chopped
- ½ lemon, juice only
- 1 cup spelt spaghetti, cooked
- 1 shallot, finely chopped
- 1 garlic clove, finely chopped
- Rocket, 1 Handful
- Spinach, 1 Handful
- Chopped chive, 1 handful
- Chopped cauliflower, 1 handful

INSTRUCTIONS:

a) Warm the coconut oil, then slowly sauté the tomatoes, shallot, and garlic.
b) Add the lemon juice.
c) Serve on top of the spaghetti.

Mushrooms & spinach

Makes: 3

NUTRITION: Calories: 179| Fat: 17g | Carbohydrates: 7g | Sugars: 1g | Protein: 3g

INGREDIENTS:

- 1 red onion, sliced
- 5-6 mushrooms, sliced
- olive oil, 2 tablespoons
- ¼ cup cherry tomatoes, sliced
- 1 clove of garlic, minced
- Pinch of ground nutmeg

- 3 cups fresh spinach, shredded
- coconut oil, 1 teaspoon
- fresh lemon juice, ½ Tablespoon
- fresh lemon zest, finely grated, 1 teaspoon
- Pinch ground black pepper
- Pinch Low-Sodium Salt

INSTRUCTIONS:

a) Sauté the mushrooms for 4 minutes in hot coconut oil. Set aside.
b) Sauté the vegetables for about three minutes in olive oil.
c) Add the tomatoes, salt, pepper, lemon zest, and garlic, and cook for 2 to 3 minutes, gently mashing the tomatoes with a spatula.
d) Cook the greens for 3 minutes or so.
e) Add the mushrooms and lemon juice, then turn off the heat and serve.

Braised Collard Greens With Pepperoncini

Makes: 10

NUTRITION: Calories 62|Fat 3g | Saturated 1g| Unsaturated 2g|Protein 3g |Carbohydrates 5g|Fiber 2g|Sugars 1g |Sodium 258mg

INGREDIENTS:

- 16-ounce package of collard greens, chopped
- chopped red onions, 1 cup
- 4 fresh thyme sprigs
- unsalted chicken stock, 2 cups
- minced garlic,1 tablespoon

- diced pancetta, 2 ounces
- undrained pickled pepperoncini slices, ¼ cup
- olive oil, 1 tablespoon
- kosher salt, ½ teaspoon

INSTRUCTIONS:

a) Combine the collard leaves, chicken stock, onions, pancetta, garlic, oil, and thyme in a 6-quart Crockpot and cook for 8 hours on medium heat.
b) Cut the thyme stems off.
c) Serve immediately with the pickled pepperoncini and salt.

Tofu and Spinach Lasagne

Makes: 2

NUTRITION: 198 Calories| Protein 8g| Carbohydrates 24g | Sugar 1 g | Fat 8g

INGREDIENTS:

- baby spinach, 2 handfuls
- soft silken tofu, 2 cups
- 8 Roma tomatoes, peeled
- 1 lemon
- 2 garlic cloves
- 1 red onion
- 1 red pepper, roasted and peeled
- Spelt Lasagne
- 1 aubergine, grilled
- fresh basil, 1 handful
- 1 courgette, grilled

INSTRUCTIONS:

a) Preheat the oven to 180 degrees Fahrenheit.
b) Blend the pepper, tomatoes, garlic clove, and basil; set aside.
c) Blend tofu, the other garlic clove, lemon juice, and spinach to make a paste.
d) To assemble the lasagne, layer the courgette and aubergine with the leftover tomatoes, tofu, and spinach combination, followed by a layer of lasagne.
e) Bake for 35 minutes.

SNACKS AND APPETIZERS

Roasted Pine Nuts

Makes: 4

NUTRITION: Calories: 188|Protein: 4 grams| Fat: 18 grams | Carbohydrates: 4 grams|Sugar: 1 g

INGREDIENTS:

• pine nuts, ¼ cup

• cold-pressed olive oil, 1 teaspoon

INSTRUCTIONS:

a) Toast the pine nuts in olive oil for 5 to 10 minutes, or until golden brown.

Veggie Sticks with Hummus

Makes: 2

NUTRITION: 26g carbohydrates|Sugar 1 g |11g fat | 6g protein |220 calories

INGREDIENTS:

• 1 carrot, sliced thin
• ½ cucumber, sliced thin
• 1 pepper, sliced thin

• 1 celery stick, sliced thin
• 1 serving hummus

INSTRUCTIONS:

a) Serve with hummus

Gingered Pecans

Makes: 4

NUTRITION: 300 Calories |18g Carbohydrates|26g Fat|4g Protein |1g Sugar

INGREDIENTS:

- Stevia, 1 packet
- cold-pressed olive oil, ½ tablespoon
- pecan halves, ½ cup
- ginger powder, ¼ teaspoon
- sea salt, ½ teaspoon
- Water, 4 tablespoons

INSTRUCTIONS:

a) Combine stevia, sea salt, and ginger in a small dish.
b) Heat the olive oil in a small saucepan, add the pecans and stevia combination, and cook while stirring frequently,
c) Layer the pecans on paper towels to dry.

Stacked Carrot & Courgette

Makes: 2

NUTRITION: 91 Calories|33g Carbohydrates|1g Fat|0 Protein|1g Sugar

INGREDIENTS:

- 1 carrot, grated
- 1 lemon
- Olive oil or avocado oil
- Sesame seeds
- baby spinach leaves, 1 handful
- 1 courgette, grated
- ½ avocado
- Quinoa, 2 servings

INSTRUCTIONS:

a) Cook the quinoa and spread it out.
b) Stack the grated carrot and courgette on top.
c) Garnish with spinach, avocado, sesame seeds, lemon juice, and olive oil.
d) Season to flavor with salt and pepper.

Sweet Potato Chips

Makes: 2

NUTRITION: Calories: 148 |Fat: 9g |Carbohydrates: 16g |Sugars: 2.5g |Protein: 0.8g.

INGREDIENTS:

- 1 tablespoon olive oil
- 1 avocado, diced
- 1 tomato, diced
- 1 sweet potato
- 1 tablespoon sesame seeds
- Paprika

INSTRUCTIONS:

a) Preheat the oven to 210 degrees Fahrenheit.
b) Wash the sweet potato well before slicing it thinly to form rough chips. Rub in olive oil and Himalayan salt.
c) Bake the chips until golden brown and crunchy.
d) In a mixing dish, combine everything.
e) When the chips are done baking, add paprika on top and top with the avocado mixture.

Fried Queso Blanco

Makes: 1

NUTRITION: 520 Calories | 43g Fats | 2g Carbohydrates |1g Sugar |30g Protein | 170mg Sodium

INGREDIENTS:

- 1 Pinch Red Pepper Flakes
- Queso Blanco cubed, 6 ounces
- Olives, 2 ounces
- Olive Oil, 1½ tablespoons

INSTRUCTIONS:

a) Heat the oil and melt the cheese cubes.
b) Continue to heat the cheese, then fold half of it in on itself.
c) Continue to flip the cheese and heat it until a beautiful crust forms.
d) Use the melted cheese to form a cube, sealing the edges with a second spatula.
e) Turn off the heat.
f) Cut into pieces and serve with pepper flakes and olive oil.

DESSERT

Tofu Lemon Pie

Makes: 4-6

NUTRITION: Calories 338| Fat 22g | Carbohydrate 28g| Protein 13g |Sugar 1 g

INGREDIENTS:

LEMON PIE FILLING
- 2 Stevia packets
- 12 ounces silken tofu, drained
- lemon zest, divided, 1½ tablespoons
- soy powder, 2 tablespoons
- Juice of 1 lemon

PIE CRUST
- psyllium powder, 1 teaspoon
- almonds, soaked overnight, 1 cup
- cold-pressed olive oil, ½ tablespoon
- Dates, ½ cup

INSTRUCTIONS:

FILLING

a) Completely blend the tofu, lemon juice, ½ tablespoon of lemon zest, and stevia in a mixer.

b) Add the soy powder gradually and blend for an additional minute.

CRUST

c) In a food blender, combine the almonds, dates, olive oil, psyllium powder, and remaining lemon zest.

d) Evenly cover the bottom and edges of the pie dish with the almond mixture by pressing firmly into place.

e) Bake for 10 to 12 minutes.

f) After the crust has chilled, fill it with the filling and smooth the top with a spatula.

g) Bake the pie for 25 to 30 minutes, or until the middle is set and the edges are lightly golden.

h) Chill the pie after letting it come to room temperature before serving.

Sugar-Free Spinach Brownies

Makes: 4

NUTRITION: Calories 114.3|Fat 8.2 g| Carbohydrate 5 g| Sugars 0.1 g | Protein 4.0 g

INGREDIENTS:

- almond oil, ½ cup
- frozen chopped spinach, 1¼ cups
- sugar-free chocolate, 6 ounces
- ½ cup almond oil 6 eggs
- a few drops of stevia
- cocoa powder, ½ cup

- 1 teaspoon vanilla pod
- the low sodium salt, ½ teaspoon
- baking soda, ¼ teaspoon
- ½ teaspoon cream of tartar
- pinch cinnamon

INSTRUCTIONS:

a) Position a baking tray lined with wax paper inside an oven and heat it to 325 degrees F.
b) Combine olive oil and chocolate to melt them. Add vanilla and stir.
c) Combine the chocolate, cinnamon, salt, baking soda, and cream of tartar.
d) Puree the greens and egg in a food processor.
e) Include almond oil in the food mixer and mix thoroughly.
f) Slowly pour the melted chocolate combination into the egg mixture while blending or processing it continuously.
g) Combine the dry ingredients and blend or whisk until completely blended.
h) Drop the ingredients into the baking dish in an even layer.
i) Bake the cake for 40 minutes, then cut it into pieces.

Sugarless Chocolate Banana Ice Cream

Makes: 2

NUTRITION: Calories: 121|Fat: 4g|Sodium: 5mg|Carbohydrates: 22g |Sugars: 0g|Protein: 3g

INGREDIENTS:

- unsweetened cocoa powder, ¼ cup
- 3 ripe bananas, sliced and frozen

- vanilla extract, 1 teaspoon
- unsweetened almond milk, ¼ cup
- Salt, ¼ teaspoon

INSTRUCTIONS:

a) Blend or process all of the components until they are thoroughly combined.
b) Spread the mixture out in a shallow container, and then freeze it for two hours.
c) To stop ice crystals from developing, scrape the ice cream with a fork every 30 minutes.
d) Once the ice cream has frozen and become fluffy, serve it right away,

Sugar-Free Chocolate Mousse

Makes: 2

NUTRITION: Calories: 180|Fat: 15g|Saturated Fat: 10g|Carbohydrates: 7g
|Sugars: 1g|Protein: 5g

INGREDIENTS:

- vanilla extract, 1 teaspoon
- 1 ripe avocado, peeled and pitted
- Pinch of sea salt
- sugar-free maple syrup, ¼ cup
- unsweetened almond milk, ½ cup
- unsweetened cocoa powder, ½ cup

INSTRUCTIONS:

a) Place all the ingredients in a food processor or blender, and process until fully creamy and smooth.
b) Transfer the mixture to a serving bowl or glass.
c) Cover and chill for a minimum of two hours, or until firm.
d) Serve chilled, and if preferred, top with chopped nuts or fresh berries.

CONCLUSIONS

In conclusion, following a low-sugar diet can help you enjoy your favorite foods to the fullest, satisfy cravings, and maintain the right blood sugar levels. Limiting your consumption of added sugars can help avoid blood sugar spikes and crashes. You may feel more energized and concentrated as a result all day long.

Additionally, if you follow a low-sugar diet, you might be able to escape the pattern of sugar cravings, which frequently results in overeating and weight gain. By zeroing in on nutrient-dense foods and reducing your intake of processed foods and sweetened beverages, you can assist your taste buds in becoming more receptive to the natural sweetness of food and a broader range of flavors and textures.

Lastly, you can aid in reducing the rate at which sugar enters your system. and feel more satiated after eating by including healthy fats, protein, and fiber in your meals and snacks. This can help you feel like you have more control over your eating and keep you from overeating or overindulging in sugary snacks.

While still allowing you to indulge in your favorite foods in moderation, a low-sugar diet can be a long-lasting and enjoyable strategy for achieving optimal health and wellness.

INDEX

A

B

C

Made in United States
Troutdale, OR
06/01/2023

10382386R00050